sugah. lump. prayer
MOMTAZA MEHRI

Published by Akashic Books
©2017 Momtaza Mehri

ISBN: 978-1-61775-571-2

Akashic Books
Brooklyn, New York
Twitter: @AkashicBooks
Facebook: AkashicBooks
E-mail: info@akashicbooks.com
Website: www.akashicbooks.com

African Poetry Book Fund
Prairie Schooner
University of Nebraska
110 Andrews Hall
Lincoln, Nebraska 68588

Table of Contents

Preface
by Tijan M. Sallah

Being of East African (Somali/Jeberti) and Yemeni descent, Momtaza Mehri is, herself, a physical expression of the Red Sea region's demographic hybridity, which plays out in *sugah. lump. prayer*, her debut chapbook collection.

sugah. lump. prayer is an iconoclastic group of poems that meanders between the sacred and secular, the transcendental and the mundane. *Sugah* functions here as a colloquial metaphor for all the delights that satiate our baser instincts, and *prayer* refers to our transcendental inclinations, our predisposition to seek spiritual solace by aligning our souls with an unfathomable mystery. The poetry collection is framed around the segments of the day which benchmark the Muslim times of prayer and all the in-situ happenings: *Fajr* (in Arabic, reference to morning prayer); *Dhuhr* (afternoon); *Asr* (late afternoon); *Maghrib* (evening), and *Isha* (night). These temporal segments are for the Muslim or believer, several times daily, to remember the Abrahamic or Ibrahimic God (*Elohim, Jehovah, Allah*) and to submit to the will of the Creator.

These poems, however, are not about dogma. In fact, it could be argued they are about the opposite. In their subversive spirit, the poems use religious ideas and images to cross all kinds of forbidden boundaries: refugees, immigrant life, love, sex, conflict, violence, and cyber interactions. The poems are elliptical; on first reading, they register as dithyrambic puzzles. In their deeper conviction, they reveal a malleable, exploratory, tender, and tolerant mind.

Take, for example, the opening poem of the collection, "Call it something other than strength," in the segment called "Fajr." Here the poem starts, "In the Name of His Name," a twist on the religious cliché "in the name of God," but the poet uses this to offer profound commentary on the sacredness of life in two beautiful lines, "In the beginning there was life, then death / . . . This order makes us who we are." In a sense, the poet in these lines calls us to conscience. Recognizing and celebrating the sanctity of life should precede and be given greater weight than concerns with death. Mehri puts it beautifully, at the poem's end: "Is there anything more morbid than a body that refuses to die? / More holy?"

Several lines in the collection stand out for their beauty and precision: "home is where the hurt is," a reference to the pains of the immigrant experience in the poem "Transatlantic (take one)"; or "His people/Her people (God aren't we a mess)," a line in "Transatlatic (take two)" that alludes to two lovers in a transatlantic, crosscultural encounter and the Manichean tensions that arise from this relationship; or in the poem "Clockwise," in which the speaker says, "I want to believe in so much more than this. I want to / say we are more than our geographies of loss," expressing elegantly the magnitude of what is lost from ill-informed reductionism of the immigrant experience; or, finally, the wisdom we find in "Answer Me This," full of lines like: "A life is never one side of a debate. I am unsure of everything but this."

The poems in this collection are idiosyncratic. Everyday images, such as coffee, pecans, maple, caramel, cocoa butter, and breakfast cereal are interspersed with violent images, as in the poem, "Grief in HTML," where the poet notes, "a window shard clarifies itself against the slackness of suit and skin, imprints into the chest of a family friend. He is flesh opening into a socket for wood chips to lodge in. He is dressed in crystals. He is dissolved." Such ugly moments call into doubt how an omnipotent and omniscient deity can allow such things to happen, and asks how sane humans can claim to be doing this in the name of what the poet calls *"yarabbyarahmaan."* How inhumanely frightening and senseless are mindless acts of terror? The poet is aghast about such violence and the effects on victims and relatives.

Mehri's collection bristles with beautiful lines reminiscent of the northern Somali *jiifto* poetry, in the way they combine modern nomadism (the immigrant experience) with addressing important political, religious, and philosophical issues. In many instances, the poems recount personal experiences or reflections, and they meander broadly and bring a collage of images—religious, political, sexual, psychosomatic, and cyber. Since many of the poems are elliptical, they are therefore not easy to give a linear interpretation. In fact, these poems capture the subversive dare of an iconoclastic imagination that leaves the reader hungry and unsettled, salivating for more. I invite you to venture into them.

you heard me singing about sorrow honey,
all the infidels know that tune,
sweet darkness left us naked at the dividing line . . .
—Akilah Oliver (1961–2011), *A Collection of Objects*

Call it something other than strength

In the Name of His Name.

I pull on a pair of gloves, acid-yellow,
wipe a plate dry,
mimic a sun, rising.

Spool back this confession of hands and warm suds,
their final touch, hiss
and pop. A droplet of tahleel spat into twin skins behind ears.
There is a violence under my nails. An elbow resting against a sink's edge, its lip
damper than an eyelid,
both hands flat, and insidious against a saucepan's bottom.

In the beginning there was life, then death. Clockwise with the sponge, don't forget.
This order makes us who we are.
We're still having the middle parts decided for us.
In the meantime, the dream time, our arrogant cells multiply
in spite of themselves, tear each other apart in their soft millions.

Is there anything more morbid than a body that refuses to die?
More holy?

buttercream bismillahs

Each morning we wake up on opposite sides of the bed
and play at being Lazarus for a day, an afternoon.
Some of us will make it back, the rest
descending into a breaking night, only to be mourned
by those who look like us
across the split lip of an ocean.

Transatlantic (take one)

i
hararehandsworthharlemhavanahejaz
hejazhavanaharlemhandsworthharare
home is where the hurt is.

ii
You, the Amreekans. Untamed, prone to
silly little things like sundown towns and genocide.
Glowing luminous in our Queen's English textbooks. Us, the lost children of
the Estuary,
needing your beacons to kindle the corners of our dark rooms.
Before that, all I could claim was the currency of expat TV channels and lost years.
Our very fabric uncoils into an exchange of hands
and drizzled hums. I think of duty free and glazed biscuits at Terminal 1,
the closest I got to tasting your lips. They don't make 'em like that in my country.
Not that one. I meant, my other country. I mean, I live the exported script.
And you? The sequel. Ain't it funny, truly yaa akhi,
how everything comes full circle?

Dhuhr

Transatlantic (take two)

We wanted a music that they couldn't play.
—Thelonious Monk on bepop (and us I think)

Over coffee and a pecan maple, they sit.
A Thursday midmorning is as good a time as any
to discuss the generational ache of
second-guessing.

A god conveniently wearing the same face, genitals
as tax collector / border guard / leering judge.
He carries a police baton / its fall is a language we both understand
though the stretch / of / syllables often differs
from shore / to / shore.

His people / Her people (God, aren't we a mess?)
Aren't they beautiful, despite everything,
or maybe because of everything? Semantics, he brushes aside crumbs, bulldozes
a heap of granulated brown.
Asks her if she knows the song they're playing right now, over speakers.

Under his place mat, a colony leaks, breaking
Tilbury dock banks.
Hers, an exiled song of hardheaded old women
and loose laughter.

They will leave soon, snake past the train station.
Stake a claim in the cities between each other's teeth,
much like the caffeine / itself
browning their grin,
much like the / fluoride / of the old city
itself.

November 1997

Hit rewind. Pause. Press. Who is she in the drenched lilac? Have we seen her be-fore? All the middle-aged ones look the same. One holds a wooden spoon above her head, strikes at drum center. A chorus sprays our air with qabiil shout-outs, and those of us born into other languages will throw our gunfingers up the only way we know how. This is where you will blanch at the shame of not getting "it." I love how honest we are with our pride. I used to hate that. The bride is doused in henna fire, hair cascading down her back like a lineage to hold us together. Her face is soft. I want it to stay like that just to prove this world wrong. This is healing. This is the exhale. I mean these are the humid nights that make leaving bearable and the old women click their tongues and the men dance in ill-fitting suits, plump uncles spilling out of camel shirts reminding me of how no bound-ary can contain us. A turmeric glow to soak the hall, wash us out of our shames, out of everything we won't admit to. Tonight is more than neutral survival, to-night is buraanbur and a smoke of voices singing of a love to bruise the lungs. I feel they are dying from it. I feel they will take me with them.

Fast forward. Catch two painted hands, gathered

and hollow,

as if in prayer.

zuhr

Dew or the wetness on a man's cheek. Find me a
distinction.

Both descend at night,

leave by morning.

I want to believe in so much more than this. I want to
say we are more than our geographies of loss

and believe it. Help me believe it.

labo

What is there to write about after exile?

After this dress of loose skin

and zip codes?

After the blue sighs of those before us?

Wait for it. Our backs straining into loaded cross-
bows,

in the meantime.

I think I'll write about the rain making an
industrial disaster

out of your neat face

and that time I used your toothbrush to fix my
baby hairs in the sink

and never told you.

saddex

Trust is a vowel sound away from power.

Trust is willing a boat to shore.

Power is not having to. Even our language mocks us.

afar

Lately, he cries in newsreels. Sometimes he calls it
inspiration.

You are too milk-fed, too hungry

for a story that isn't yours. The generation birthed from a
roll of dice

carving poetry out of

a blood brother's rib.

Cain translating for Abel,

a digital age away.

shan

Morning papers say debris has washed up on the coastline,

and I do not know if they mean plastic or flesh.

Some of us blur these lines.

We, who live outside the membrane of being,

beyond articulation,

inside the hum of our nightly prayers,

everything we are fearful of has already happened. Is already happening.

I couldn't tell you all the ways

land imprints on a body,

on a memory,

but each dollar sent back home carries a watermark I can't ignore.

This sea has always swallowed us,

boats have always failed us,

land has always meant barbed wire and queuing and contributing and contributing

and contributing

until the pillar-box red gloss of documentation

lends us a humanity our fathers never had.

Shouldn't we be grateful, brother?

At least, for this?

Breathe across a telephone line,

dream to cast this currency, this birthright forth at an uncle's feet. Know I do
not mean to.

Know this is what they named "luck."

<p>Grief in HTML</p>

060 112 062 071 114 105 101 102 032 105 110 032 072 084 077 076 060

<p>The bomb explodes near the central compound, makes a wheezing child-sound.</p>

<p>It's a Monday afternoon. A city sleeps on its side. Death is an ellipsis. Gasoline, cobalt, concrete, yarabbyarahmaan, a window shard clarifies itself against the slackness of suit and skin, imprints into the chest of a family friend. He is flesh made rapture. He is dressed in crystals. He is dissolved.</p>

<p>A father on the other side of a glass screen logs in. Facebook. His eyes their own brand of muddy blue longing. Five years since, his friend is still a life undeleted, peering from under horn-rimmed glasses. Four walls of a coffin or the four walls of a display picture? Find me the difference. A man shifts in a quasi-dream called afterlife.</p>

<p>My father's cuff links, cold and dulled, on a drawer desk a dead man bought him for a wedding gift. The heat of a pavement turns xalwo into caramel into plasma.</p>

<p>The old poets said home was a woman. Only a woman can bleed this much without dying. Maybe home is a man's lust ticking under a vest, leaving us to pick up the pieces.</p>

<p>Imagine a rage that needs to spread like that?</p>

Transatlantic (take three)

iii

A mother's lip liner shrieking from the first photo of the lost album: The Giza
   Years.

The color of kidney beans left out in a dying sun. I feed the ducks and watch a
   kinder,

more tolerant sun melt Streatham Common into Gramercy Park groves, a
   cowlick away.

They say we all eventually turn into our mothers.

In both versions, the air carries our sighs to a place where they won't be trans-
   lated as

ungratefulness.

iv

There's this Basquiat painting of a black skeleton riding a white one.

Riding with Death, he called it.

A gorgeous cloud of dismemberment. I still haven't figured out why the
   apocalypse looks like a tango.

Or why the white one wears a leash.

v

Sugarcane under fingernails, a shut door,

a schoolboy's teeth scraping against ink boots,

a spiraled kink behind each ear,

and this foundation stone (upon this Pete Rock we built this fat beat)

made all this holy

out of our grief's commonality.

The Sag

Cumar's sirwaal is ever-baggy. Pick it up, Mama would say. Waryaa, you look like a street boy on heat. You've made a falling sunset out of CK drawers.

He would argue, until the reach of her hands proved fatal. Hook each finger inside a denim loop, lifting upward. The sky hoisted up on the seventh day. Pull up your pants and they won't shoot. Pull up your pants, turn Mohammed into Mo. Remind him he is no longer boy. Was never, will never be boy enough, small enough.

His indignant breath rising and falling, one lined hand flattened against a back. Bear with her. This, the only thing she can straighten out. His belt now linear, a careful underline.

Be rigid, for now. Make the bridge of a spine your very own siraatulmustaqeem.

Lauryn sang it, straight from the book. Shot it straight from the hip.

Do it for me.

Do it for us.

I believe in the transformative power of cocoa butter and breakfast cereal in the afternoon

Pick a sky and name it. The scriptures say there are seven.
We have enough time.
A fig, bruised pink, resting on the dashboard,
tilted as if to say,
Khalaas, get it over with, naayaa.

This breeze feels too much like an aunt, tugging at our scalps,
hardly saying sorry. I think of how perfectly
timed your buzzcut is. How the border was dotted with goats,
lone whistle-blowers against concrete skyscrapers.
Here, in the country of your birth, we cross the Persian Gulf,
leaving a lush behind us, and the stark of my bracelets,
green as Uganda.

A tunnel above us, reflected in a lucent drop
of light on your cheek. This liminal state between island and man.
Between Africa and the Peninsula,
the world's two thick thighs,
or heartbreaks.

Behind us, they are drinking from time's cup,
under the same stars a prophet gazed up
at. They call them drones now. I think. Ahead,
I know even less,
except our feet hanging off a hotel bed;
a geologic upheaval.

Your mother sits in the glove compartment, the kohl shedding
from her eyes.
I share you with her,
the way we share our unbelonging
and make a castle out of
this bottled sigh
they call living.

I believe in a place where we can be ugly and poor and needy
and still wear crowns.
Take me there.

Maghrib

In that order

my body gives way to salt gives way to a bruised telephone line gives way to hon-eyed mahalibya tones gives way to the corner of your mouth gives way to I can smell it on you gives way to that russet-mustached soldier on the cheapest stamp gives way to the letters gives way to burnt sukkar gives way to caramel ripple gives way to slipping on cotton socks gives way to slippery men gives way to

dissolve

A Mars bar connects the dots where our skin burnt the map

a night unfurls into gold.   a galaxy bopping its heavy head.
the tinge of a planet unwrapped.   one day, a man's glucose levels spike
into catastrophe.   a twenty-three-year-old is told a knife was
driven into his father's head,   a sea away, or a lifetime. the war meant
little to him before that.   it never means anything until it does.

now, it numbs his tongue to anything other than imported beans.
he sleeps alone, to the sound of a microwave, turning a solid bar on its side,
a dervish in gooey slow motion. i roll my neck backward through time,
hear its plastic foil shrivel in mock protest.

years later, my father tells me diabetes runs in the family.
i do not ask him if it was on purpose,   this enforced diet of caramel
and dearth. if cocoa, bitter, was his   attempt at returning home
to a soil darker (or wetter)   than the one he left.

Isha

"... and make loose the knot from my tongue"

some days this bed is so big I drown in it.
some days I fold inward into a sac of flesh, sealed.

behind each knee is a militarized region,

skin soft as a plum, a Green Zone of its own, each thigh a teardrop held steady.
make me steady.

a singular lost sock under a rusting frame, bunsen-blue. meaning I've been
trying to find that thing that used to fit, the way I could reach under so much
easier back then.

my arms got a lot bigger since, and my hands, each palm a hollow. nah call it
a catcher's mitt to that drowning man bopping at your throat. a sweat bead
swings from each earlobe, ghee-thick.

*

pomegranate-rindboy.

the kind of stateless I like. the kind that always finds me. hunger is each hair lifted
at the nape. or my grandfather's parietal lobe staining the welcome rug. some
kind of offering. it isn't fair, walaalo, it ain't. but we must have been last in line
when fair was being handed out. or else we'd have a belly full of something more
than newspaper clippings. i mean you're gonna be a headline anyway, mightas-
well make a meal of it. mightaswell scratch and burp and fart.

If He Wills It

one day I'm gonna grab this horizon by its belt but a boy named Anwar with a freshly scraped scalp leaning against an exit sign seems enough. for now. and he's gonna make me fuller than a pregnant moon.

or two.

*

Choices

for Xashi Ali Saleh

I've seen a man die slowly and call it fatherhood.

Lord, do not impose upon us one who does not fear You.

Too much caano iyo subug, that's your problem, you think too much qul khairan aw asmut there are no awards for carrying wars in your stomach for dreaming yourself into my heartbreaks I broke my back to give you all this language you use to tell me all the ways I have failed.

Our grandfather was the wrong tribe is there a right one I don't know they burst in startled the tusbax out of his hands maybe they questioned him first maybe he answered maybe it was a misunderstanding the way a bullet mistakes a frontal lobe for a homecoming the way his organs made a weeping sunrise of the walls behind him the way I use his death to lend me a lil' depth the way I can't not bear witness the way no one asked me to.

I cough twice.

Remove him utterly.

Manifesto For Those Carrying Dusk Under Their Eyes

Leave the eggs sunny-side up next to khaala's beetroot jam jars and ice-cream tubs, bambara bean-filled and flatulent. Here, no one calls you brave, or articulate. Here, you speak like you were born here because you were. There is nothing extraordinary about that. The lash of the old regime lines your neighbor's back, and no, you won't write about that. Those old poems drip with musk and Spotify will not categorize them as "World Music" because, well, aren't we the world? Aren't we small enough to disappear when we want to?

Aren't we enough?

A sprig of rayhaan, attar-doused and jummah prayers and feet washed in the sink. No, there ain't nothing disgusting about that and if you think so, you can fuck yourself on plush Egyptian cotton. I mean, I already got the armor. Twin warheads otherwise named eyebrows and wallahi I've learned to raise them. Higher than the sky hanging from its hinge, higher still

and rising,

rising,

rising.

Answer Me This

A bag of flesh and squamous cells is not a walking headline.
A chin turned upward is just a chin, not a question mark, hardly ever a prayer.
A digitalised 32-page document is a gateway
into the territory marked *HUMAN,*
block capitals brand a birthplace.
Wear it like it fits. Even if it doesn't.

I didn't ask for any of it. No one gave me a choice.
Maybe the choice lies in the biometrics of a fingerprint,
the day I breached a mother's waters on this side of the ambit.

A life is never one side of a debate. I am unsure of everything but this.
The left side of the heart is bigger.

That doesn't make it more truthful.

To Him We Belong

Tonight, I will settle for comfortable, which looks a lot like selfish
or myopic or a girl-turned-rage-turned-nobody
dressed in faux-chinchilla and kitten pumps in the queue for a kebab at 2 a.m.
I'm gonna do my best impression of a long river running,
of a final gasp, a meaty bass line.
I'll lick the sweat on each forearm, each bruise
a blush of memory.

 If I can't have this beauty, let me have namelessness.
 At least then, I can name my dead in the kind of peace they deserved.

This is the part where I live for those before me,
scratch my name into this gun-named street,
behind the twice-named church,
and call it a return.

and to Him we will return

ACKNOWLEDGMENTS

"I believe in the transformative power of cocoa butter and breakfast cereal in the afternoon" first appeared in *Puerto Del Sol, 2016*. This piece was short-listed for the Plough Poetry Prize.
"The Sag" first appeared in *Elsewhere: A Journal of Place*.
Excerpts from "Clockwise" were first published as "New World Hymn" in *Brittle Paper*.

THE HABITUAL BE
CHIMWEMWE UNDI

Published by Akashic Books
©2017 Chimwemwe Undi

ISBN: 978-1-61775-568-2

Akashic Books
Brooklyn, New York
Twitter: @AkashicBooks
Facebook: AkashicBooks
E-mail: info@akashicbooks.com
Website: www.akashicbooks.com

African Poetry Book Fund
Prairie Schooner
University of Nebraska
110 Andrews Hall
Lincoln, Nebraska 68588

TABLE OF CONTENTS

PREFACE
by Tsitsi Jaji

Years ago, a language teacher introduced the "habitual present" as the tense of thoughtless acts—*I come, I go, I look, I eat, I read, I write. I forget to notice.* Chimwemwe Undi is a poet interested in breaking our bad habit of living as if life could go on without us, without us noticing. In many of her poems, that *us* coheres in memory, and it is remembering together what water, or fruit, or dance felt like that brings Undi's chorus into being. If habits turn the daily into drab drudgery, these poems are, like the shards of a broken cup, "mended with gold," here to glint light into the small, strange beauty of the every day. Undi invites her readers to "Check our iterative existence, our defiant glory / the way we are and are and are / and be."

This collection plays with several iterations of what glory is made of. It opens by tripping over the grammar of racialized violence: if *grief* is a noun, *grieving* is a verb. "Listing (v.)" keens, lurching into the slant truths of repeating news of Black people dying. "Say her name" has become all too familiar a mantra in North America, and Undi's words stumble over the impulse toward a litany of memorials, demanding we pay attention by "having trouble remembering." The legacies of other necessary acts of survival resonate in the poem's open-endedness, in the maps and archives on its edges.

These are poems to break a spell. Investigating the roots of her own syntax, Undi traces how Southern African English echoes the cadences of the church. Without spelling out the politics of language, she airs an idiom inflected by former president Frederick Chiluba's 1991 official declaration that Zambia was a Christian nation. But her words rephrase this legacy: she keeps prayer's posture, inclined toward revelations of wonder in the ordinary, while shaking off its pieties:

> There's something bred into those of us
> raised in chapels and Sunday best

(something beaten gently in)
that makes us seek holiness in
whatever might hold it.

Throughout this book the ordinary stuff of life matters—a comb working through kinky hair, illicit cigarettes, a secret recipe casserole—and the direction of reverence proves as malleable as copper, and as quick to burnish the dull into something lustrous.

In her poems, Undi also evidences a spoken-word artist's savoring of the sonic. Alliteration, internal rhymes, and a sure meter wear on the line's surface that beautiful struggle to liberate the word, disavow naming's will to ossify meaning, yet bearing witness to its violent turns:

(Here is a secret about burning.)
It is happening all the time
Even when you are not looking.
Even when you believe the bliss-filled rumors
and the whispers about pillars of salt
demonize the space above your left shoulder.

These poems also bear witness to Southern Africans' deep histories of itinerate being. Herdsmen, forcibly evicted famers, migrant laborers, political and economic refugees, and those who simply choose to move, haunt the "history of houses built out of spite." They watch how those moves are navigated—a "mother stops watching the news . . . because it makes her heart hurt and her teeth ache," a daughter notices what seems like apathy with narrowing eyes: "all of a sudden we are the silent faces who turned up the Afrikaans radio and ignored the screaming from the streets." In this exacting attention to complexity, this work traces patterns between overwhelming injustices "back home" and the tricky morality of settling (in) a new home, on land that was itself expropriated from First Nations, as when a father wryly notes history's rhymes: "Anishinaabe sounds African."

In the midst of such a rigorous ethic, Undi revels in the sensuality of life's sticky, sweaty seams. She celebrates with Lucille Clifton the survival of Black womanhood by centering the "dark perfection" of the body. To love is to linger over a "knot between your shoulder blades" or "the loose skin of a neck"; to recover is to linger in the earthy materialities of blood, fingernails, teeth. Her words bare the psychic costs of staying alive in Black bodies subject to an entire globe's variations on predation by calling us to "resist holiness" and its foreswearing of this here, this now. Instead these poems command us to "flourish," we imminent incarnations of Being. That action, she argues, takes courage when:

> I am too careless with myself,
> too aware that death does not feel like an end to me,
> and neither like a door,
> but like an empty bus seat
> exactly when my feet are tired.

The intimacy of *The Habitual Be's* relationships—family, friends, and lovers—draws us into feeling its political exigencies. This collection's urgency is firmly anchored in the mundane losses of our present moment. Undi knows our habits of attention. The hundreds drowned in a boat crossing from Libya to Lampedusa hardly make the news. Sinkane's diasporic song "How We Be" cannot move us to grieve the mounting toll of renewed violence in South Sudan. The violences done to women are so mundane that South Africa reelects a rapist as president. But these are both new and old sorrows, and we have been breaking them by inhabiting and thus hallowing our own bodies. It is a call we have heard before, including from Keorapetse Kgositsile, South Africa's poet laureate.

Undi's poems transform desire into memory, and the *Habitual Be* makes our living lovely over and over and over again . . . the every day of regular folk, made paramount.

LISTING (V.)

In dog years, I am dead. In Black years, alive,
so: exceptional, increasingly so. I ask strangers
for directions on pocket scraps & build myself
a map home as cohesive as a litany
I am having trouble remembering.

I am having trouble remembering.
There are too many bodies in this room built for bodies.
We are magic typecast as disappearing acts, history
whispered into memories.

& easier things:
1. the prime ministers in chronological order,
2. My Very Educated Mother Just Served Us Nachos,
3. the angle at which the earth leans, shaking us off like water.

There is too much to say
for this mouth built for praying.
There are too many names to unhear
so I don't have to remember
or truly, repeat to meaninglessness,
or truly, forget them,
outrage a poor mnemonic device.

I am having trouble remembering.
I am forgetting & that is the worst part.
I cannot hold a name long enough
to know it. Even the faces are growing statistical,
the write-ups into archives. I know guilt better

than grief, as well as a restlessness,
better than a Black body breathing still.

4C

Cornered laughter not malicious but indifferent.
Still big & clear enough to see myself inside.

My mothers gather in kitchens & grip each other
between their knees, suffer small agonies,

preventative medicine: better to ache in the arms
of a loved one than to ask a stranger what they

mean by the word. Sore hidden among baby hair
like a little treasure, & a box of broken ties,

& a comb unsmiling. My face is tight from giggling
& from dried tears where the hands did not relent

in hanging me by my prison. This dark pride.
Hands linked & curled around themselves.

I am tender-headed to match my engine.
My type is some prophesy,

reads:
Apply heat to heavy dark & weave fabric to wash out back. Long
     murk, starless evening,
washcloths & basin, ashy knees & soles burning from the trapped
     light that warms the earth.
Fashion from this a hammock, or a life (one that feels like the other
     (almost).

Good hair,
as in God hair,
as in if you pray to it
you'll have an easier time in most rooms.

PSALM READING

Faith holds fast to what is good
or what's available.

In the clearing behind our church,
the nearly lapsed smoke cigarettes like
it might save them and
your gay cousin with all the piercings
does tarot readings at birthday parties now.

There's something bred into those of us
raised in chapels and Sunday best
(something beaten gently in)
that makes us seek holiness in
whatever might hold it.

The winter god abandoned me,
it barely snowed and
I hung divine significance
in the gnashing teeth of every
new absence,
every abyss was staring me down
and singing.

When I stopped feeling
everything I thought was everything
warm and sighing by my shoulder,
I first transferred devotion
to the absence of Him,
and found that Nothing,

in all its weightless unknowing,
was precisely what I deserved.
No god could beckon as beautifully.
No god has the sharp-fanged swagger of a gap,
with its thirsty mouth
awaiting whatever needs to be held.

I have forgotten
how to hold things sacred,
so I'm practicing on horoscopes and tarot cards
and people who laugh when they're nervous.

I am too careless with myself,
too aware that death does not feel like an end to me,
and neither like a door,
but like an empty bus seat
exactly when my feet are tired.

I wonder less if
God could build a rock too heavy for His hands,
and more if life would smirk the same
if I left it,
if it would glimmer with that wet-eyed
empty sentimentality that goodbyes demand.

This new thought experiment
has me packing up all my belongings
into boxes
just to see what it would look like.

This misses the days when I thought the earth

was hollow at its core,
took comfort in wondering
what it would sound like
when my ghost echoed
in all that
space.

MZUNGU

Your vapid, gaping mouth
a site of sixteen sundry desires,
mine agape. Bespectacled, Black,
besotted. Bathed in electronic incandescence
in the sacred bedroom of girlhood,
founding wistfulness inside of me,
a new, unshakable vice.

Other bodies wonderlands,
mine a hell-scape, a veld both under fire
& unworthy of light, pitch with forgotten heat.
When you baptize your crotch
my unholy saboteur, I forget
how you loved me,
how you disregard the unchecked fervor
of an adolescent heart,
of the eighth-row sing-along,
of permanency pierced by
flesh-earned flippancy,
the ease with which you string up history
like adornments in store windows.

I wish I did not crave
your flood of fluorescence,
that white light,
the only one I ever saw.
Once, I was convinced that excess love would be the worst of it,
that my beloved would reject the deluge.
Once, I was better at loving you

& your kind, and heartbroken for easier reasons.
I was not so practiced
at climbing willingly out of a poisonous love,
pretending its cessation
had not harmed me.

SEPARATION ANXIETY

That summer,
when everything went sticky,
& we wet the fronts of our faces with the green hose in your long
garden,
& it felt like we did then,
so much mess & still thirsty.

I should have gone home six times
(I counted), but I sat on the floor by your tall lamp,
watched young fingers fight each other,
& thought, *If this is what it feels like,*
I'll try math.

That summer, love began to feel like trying when it was supposed to be
                                    breath.
Neither of us howled,
just hurt,
quiet,
the air throbbing like a vein.

That summer,
when everything went sticky,
even the air grew hands to catch us
& all the ways we were not
falling.

We pulled the hours into warm agonies,
painted the space between us,
& we could not bring ourselves to touch

while we watched it change color.

I would catch myself staring
at the knot between your shoulder blades.
We passed in the bedroom like strangers on a sidewalk
when you used to touch my back.
My love for you ached
in the wrong part of my body.

& I carried this runt between my teeth,
by the loose skin of a neck,
could not bring myself to care for it,
sensing as I did its death.

SANGENA

My grandparents' house is too small on too much land that doesn't grow much and bleeds when turned. The corn and kale that struggle from the soil are fine though. It feeds 13 children for twice as many years.

There's a truck whose bed we throw mango seeds onto from my grandparents' back porch, exactly where the seeds cannot grow, only dry and rot in the sun. The uncle who can make it go went with his mouth open, teeth gleaming, screaming in a language my teachers wouldn't let me speak.

I rebuild my mouth to look like everyone else's: faster and less foreign and standing flat-footed, trying desperately to push against the dirt I was made from. I am Black because I come from the earth's inside and I am trying to relearn the way I draw my breath so I can pretend I am not gasping.

My father says (laughing) that Anishinaabe sounds African, and wonders if the hunger growing in Chief Theresa Spence has the same desperate hands that those 300 angry prisoners in 1989 Johannesburg clenched into tired fists, and why should it be different? What is different? There is so much about the news that is too familiar to him and not familiar enough to me.

This country yelled frantic for our freedom with its own children squirming underfoot, as though its own Indian Act was no blueprint for apartheid, as though its bloodied hands were not guiding the ones that harmed us, and in homeroom I ignore these bullshit policies and marble-mouthed apologies, these things I do not know and am never taught, to sing of this true north, of strength, of freedom.

When my mother stops watching the news she says it's because it makes her heart hurt and her teeth ache, and nothing about how it is easier to smile around the water cooler and sleep at night. And all of a sudden we are the silent faces who turned up the Afrikaans radio and ignored the screaming from the streets. Suddenly we are turning two blind eyes and pretending that they are blue. Suddenly we are speaking English at the dinner table and not at all about how much this struggle looks like my uncle's open mouth, all teeth and forbidden.

My parents build a house, and it's too big on too little land they never use. They do not plant corn or kale, afraid that anything we bite into will fill our mouths with blood, and not even our own, and there is too much red already in our silent mouths.

HOW TO BE BEST FRIENDS WITH JESUS

after Ellen White's Steps to Christ

If overcome by the enemy,
cast off,
forsaken and rejected at the right hand of God,
make intercession for the beloved
sin,
advocate for the self.
He desires to restore purity and holiness,
but if you yield yourself to Him,
carry forward,
pray more fervently,
believe more fully,
you will distrust our own power.

The closer you come to Jesus,
the more faulty you will appear in your own eyes,
your imperfections broad & distinct
evidence that Satan is arousing
your deep-seated love for sinfulness.
The soul that admires divine character
but owns moral deformity
offers unmistakable evidence of ourselves.

The less we see in ourselves
the more we see in the infinite,
the soul, realizing its helplessness
reaches out.
Our sense of need drives the more exalted,
the change of heart
by which we become children.

The good seeds sewn as newborn babes
grow up,
bring forth fruit,
become mysterious trees,
illustrations of truth.

Consider the lilies,
not their anxiety but their growth,
living in this matchless encircled world,
bright in symmetry,
the likeness of nothing,
a holy life of fruitfulness.

Resist holiness.
Flourish.

A HISTORY OF HOUSES BUILT OUT OF SPITE

none of us know Amy personally, but she's here & she's singing / rising above our sodden heads bowed in something like prayer / maybe // most of us are trying to move enough to pretend she doesn't remind us of our mothers & sunday-morning spring cleans / the sharp bleached smell of it, the shrill peak of their voices demanding something far less beautiful // we're trying not / to think of mothers who mostly whisper now // or girls who looked away & uninvited us from sleepovers // even though they were smiling the whole time, or the last time that we were here / how it felt the same when we got home after // *it* as in *everything* // *the same* as in worse / you gotta move sometimes / when you're stuck in the middle of it, that's the philosophy we're buying into here / using drink tickets we bought at the dollar store & / tucked into bras & ace bandages & sagging back pockets // you gotta move // your body a last resort / occupying unceded space // the only thing that's ever belonged to you & half the girls here have called that into question // girls only because that's how you get in here / in here just because of the girls / because here is nowhere & here lives the only god that thinks our wetness akin to holy water / that answers / to the tense-bodied hallelujahs escaping mouths we thought / had forgotten how to form them // us broken daughters & all our pieces jangling // all strobe light, sweat & saxophone // when Amy died / we danced off the sorrow we knew / our mothers would shed / split their self-satisfied smugness // between us like a quarter // we tucked a backbeat under / a promise of an always love / used those tickets to buy into that sacred oath in mezzo-soprano // & we moved to it, right into it // 'cause that's what the fuck you do // our love been a losing game, Amy // we know the power of no / no // no // even when it was the wrong thing / & we know we belong here / maybe not everywhere / but that's what nowhere is for / & here we are / in the middle of it // besides / it's different for us / *us* as in   *everyone* // *different* as in   *the same.*

ON SICKNESS

after Lucille Clifton

For a month,
there is red clay in secret places
that I touch then wash
from behind the fingernails
I use to scratch my teeth.
Eventually I inquire,
find inside of myself a dead thing
I never knew was alive.

Loss
with her open mouth,
with her slow start and strident summation,
the way she conducts all my hollow spaces
so they howl in harmony,
curlicues inside of me,
falls asleep.

The dark perfection of this body
is disallowed from cracking.
Won't you celebrate with me,
nonwhite & woman, how
I can but may not name
the thing I know is
trying to kill me.

I am
the furthest thing from
a reliable witness

to the unfolding disaster
of my own biology
as evidenced
by the two soft mounds of
hysteria blooming on my
chest.

EX CAUCASIA

Some bodies are just better kindling,[1]
crave the flame. Tongues of firecracker two-step
moving through the night the way a spark does.
Too easy.
Lives laced with gasoline.[2]
Too much like soot and cargo,
nothing like you are used to,
those gaping mouths you feed
your secret-recipe casserole
at Sunday dinner.

(Here is a secret about burning.)
It is happening all the time.[3]
Even when you are not looking.
Even when you believe the bliss-filled rumors
and the whispers about pillars of salt
demonize the space above your left shoulder.

Request the light: unheavy, undark.
Stop asking me.
Ask time.[4]
Ask the years to haul their heads back above water
to briefly overcome their heaviness to tell you
why they sink so willingly out of sight.

---

1   I don't know why.
2   I don't know if.
3   I don't know where.
4   No one knows how.

ON NAMING

after Audre Lorde

Trace new fingers over glossy pictures
& rename ourselves:
cirrus, mitochondria, metamorphosis,
the gaps between shoulders
where our faces do not peer out.
Audre names our magic unwritten,
so we press desperate hands
onto pages, pretend sweat stains
into story.

In the movies with the maids
we are reminded we loved our lower place
Stratus, maybe. Fog. In that book of hymns,
proud Mary is on her knees,
Jesus has a lace front, there are
several dead animals.
In the February calendar we go over once,
the inventors of crossed roads & CCTV
& caller ID & the cataract laserphaco probe
are all pictured in closed-mouth smiles.

Close your eyes & remember us
in the future. Audre names us not
meant to survive but so far, so good.
Dead at the hands of forgotten names
that never echo in the broken spaces
they have yelled themselves into.
All the pressed skirts they ruffled.

All the anniversaries we shout down
with question marks:

Where were we, the powerhouse of the cell,
picket signs gripped & black bodies
in the kitchen? The story goes.

I am saying a thing that
has already been said:
We howled ourselves out of the margins
& into illustrations,
reclaimed the cool bleached air.
Audre names us coal & like hardness
we invented ourselves, traced back
to translucent stories opaque in the dark,
& even backward we matter. Even
in the remembered victories
of the also-forgotten,
us made twice another
were there & still are,
& still screaming,
& this isn't enough for anybody
but is something, at least.

THE HABITUAL BE

Of course we come together different,
found a better way to separate this breath
from our bad habit of living, to name a
circle a circle and disregard a line.
Of course we're mended with gold,
we're made from it. Take our new shards
and tint our laughter all yellow,
bust through paper bags.

Remember when the water crept up
& drowned all the sinners
& God made a promise we keep tempting Them to break?
Remember the fruit, how good it tasted,
how it reminded us what else our holy mouths
were for? O hell yes!
We were built to remember,
to walk on water and right on through it,
to swallow the moon and swear we're still hungry.
The language is a dance we know all the steps to.
We conjugated a life into a second coming,
and then another,
then a fourth,
endless forth.
Our mouths remember themselves, electric sliding
tongue, sampling history like soul beat. Forget you
know all the moves until the music starts.
And of course,
of course we are built of memory,
threatened to become nothing but,

but stay knowing
to double a negative does not turn it yes.

Check our iterative existence, our defiant glory,
the way we are and are and are
and be.

ACKNOWLEDGMENTS

"Listing (v.)" first appeared in *Room* magazine

"Separation Anxiety" first appeared in the *Winnipeg Free Press*

"Sangena" first appeared in *Prairie Fire Magazine*

An earlier version of "A History of Houses Built out of Spite" appeared in *The Rusty Toque*

"On Naming" first appeared in *Prairie Fire*

SABBATICAL
FAMIA NKANSA

This is a work of fiction. All names, characters, places, and incidents are a product of the author's imagination. Any resemblance to real events or persons, living or dead, is entirely coincidental.

Published by Akashic Books
©2017 Famia Nkansa

ISBN: 978-1-61775-570-5

Akashic Books
Brooklyn, New York
Twitter: @AkashicBooks
Facebook: AkashicBooks
E-mail: info@akashicbooks.com
Website: www.akashicbooks.com

African Poetry Book Fund
Prairie Schooner
University of Nebraska
110 Andrews Hall
Lincoln, Nebraska 68588

TABLE OF CONTENTS

PREFACE
by Kwame Dawes

The body that we encounter at the end of Ghanaian poet Famia Nkansa's *Sabbatical* has been transformed. "I have / crawled inside my bones," she says, "and spun a silkworm's cocoon." One imagines that we have arrived at a moment of tragedy, but this is the beginning of her recognition of the body, and her recognition, too, of what trauma, migration, chronic sickness, and the rupture of family life can do to the body of black immigrant women.

It is tempting to read these poems as pure "memoir," but Nkansa offers enough range and complexity to allow us to see that she is creating what she has described to me as a "a pastiche of what happens when Africans leave home to be 'educated.'" Without announcing it, she has constructed a persona who is best read as an amalgamation of many women. The cost of the first person, of course, is that one might be tempted to read these as poems about Nkansa herself. I have preferred to read her willingness to take this risk as an act of empathy, one prompted by the impulse to intensify the emotional weight of the collection.

In many ways, the final passage of "Moses" is an answer to the uncertainty announced at the beginning of the collection, when the speaker has declared the narrative a "new Middle Passage":

> then felt a shame thicker than sap.
> I was not kidnapped
> or sold. I was banished out of love
> so I could be molded
> and returned. Now I am back.
> Silence snores in every room.

It is a Middle Passage that helps her to understand what has haunted her as an Ewe-speaking Ghanaian woman living in America, a woman acutely

4

aware of her body's color. As she explains in her poem "The Sweetness of Juice," "my skin is dark wood, made for windowsills, never for / windows." It is this search to reconcile the crisis of her Africanness that she sets up in the opening poem of the collection, wryly called "Welcome." "I am trying to explain my intact clitoris," she writes, and then later asks the question, "Why / have I never seen a war?" Her African identity must contend with the cliché of an Africa caught in the soundtrack of *The Lion King*, and the narratives of place that do not correspond with her own life. Importantly, though, Nkansa is not suggesting that the speaker is free of many of the complexities of being an African woman in America. Indeed, in several of the poems, she unveils the internal struggle that a black woman may feel while in a sexual relationship with someone who is white. Despite the wonderful sensuality of many of these passages, there is a haunting sense that the difference is never far from the surface of things: "I am gauze. I am soot, / our thighs are glued / like tape to paper. / I clench my buttocks, / lock my legs, / hoover him in." ("Choice")

Ultimately, the duality of her feelings in these relationships will leave us with the sense that they are doomed: "Bile is pooling on my tongue. / Glee is sliding down my throat."

Slowly, Nkansa takes us further into the personal stories of the immigrant woman's life, and we recognize in her sense of irony an ability as a poet to carry multiple contradictory ideas at the same time. Even as she contemplates the presumed judgment of Kwame Nkrumah, whose frown her speaker sees for the first time after her white lover is inside her, she is also working through her sense of abandonment and the attendant mental trauma that settles in her as she considers why this relationship is not working.

It is remarkable just how many varied stories and voices Famia Nkansa compacts inside this tightly shaped gathering of poems without ever truly suggesting narrative. For her, time is fluid, and she avoids a linear engagement with when things do or do not happen. Apart from her resignation to the fact that everything will be complicated and contradicted by the next thing, very little is resolved. This quality of open questioning and voracious fascination with the unknowable turns out to be quite contagious—the disquiet and the lack of absolute clarity that marks these poems offers a kind of comfort.

Still we leave with a sense of having been let into her apartment, her world, in which her body, fully seen, reveals so much about her. In this sense, the questions she asks in "it is from my need to matter that I ask you this" are not rhetorical, but deeply felt.

The speakers in her poems contend with multiple, conflicting memories. It is clear that Nkansa is exploring the invention of narrative and voice as she uses the intimacy of the first person to construct narratives that explore issues that speak to her life and quite likely to the lives of other women. Illness, trauma, abuse, complex relationships, loss, fear, and racial dynamics are the "headline" themes that she tackles, but her use of the language of persona allows her to turn these subjects into compelling poems. So that when she speaks of the quest for mother in "Moses," for instance, we understand that it is a quest for the "mother factor" that shapes the lives of many black immigrant women:

> That time on the bus I followed a woman
> all the way to another state
> because she looked like someone
> who sold groundnuts on our street.

By the time we read these lines, we are somewhat anchored by a vague awareness that at least some of what she is searching for, in what is largely a state of mental strain, is not merely a sense of a geographical or cultural home brought on by the alienation of migration, but for a mother. This is the elusive "mother factor" who, we learn in terse, harrowing poem "Mah-Mah" (a poem likely about a grandmother figure), left, and in the process "took the starch out of / the fufu." The speaker attempts to assert her capacity to survive, to defy the loss. "I / never really liked / fufu anyway," she says, even as she declares that she, unlike Lot's wife, will not turn to salt. Yet this collection is an act of looking back.

Famia Nkansa's collection is something of a sabbatical, a place for reflection and rejuvenation, but it is one that must be productive. It must allow her to walk away from the "time off" with something to show for it. The danger of this reading of her work is that it focuses so heavily on the themes that are so deliciously present to us without, perhaps, paying sufficient attention to how fine-tuned Nkansa's poetic skills are. She eschews the cliché, she is not afraid of leaps of metaphor and image that unsettle us, and she has a splendid ear for the music of assonance and alliteration all the way through. Her allusions are employed with subtlety such that we are never left out in the cold. Instead, we have the sense that digging deeper will reward the time and effort.

WELCOME

I am trying to explain my intact clitoris,
the Jill Scott nestling against Obrafour
in a crevice of the shelf.
Nants ingonyama bagithi Baba
Gray eyes turn to slate. I cannot translate
the song. I've never fought for the right
to put the water basin down.

I stretch to steal the pencil,
so I can grab the sketchbook,
draw myself, angle my chin,
shade in my arch. They hold
both above my grasp. Why
have I never seen a war? Is my
family civilized or tribal?

CHOICE

The first time he is inside me,
Kwame Nkrumah's paper face
wears a frown I didn't see
the day before.

I am gauze. I am soot,
our thighs are glued
like tape to paper.
I clench my buttocks,
lock my legs,
hoover him in.

The Subaru cruises
through the hills,
our fingers married
around the gearshift.
His eyelashes beat like yellow wings.

My clothes squish at his glance.
A spoon is scraping against the side
of the cauldron in my ribs.
There froths
my soupy love,
the bubbling hymn
of run and stay.

Bile is pooling on my tongue.
Glee is sliding down my throat.

AFTERMATH

You have no clothes on. I do.
A Scottish skirt—the bottom half
of the schoolgirl thing we do.
Your mother said that I was cute.
It let me know she is both perplexed and proud
she raised the kind of child
who could think
I was attractive.

It's with us in the bed again, the hiss:
I will not let myself go
enough to come.
You won't pay enough attention
not to too soon.
My coming has become
another "A" we have to earn,
a relationship cliché
that should be so beneath
our two-toned love.

I can tell you're counting through
the offensive lineup of the Redskins,
one by one, one by one, to stem your tide.
I am deciding between Merlot
and a potted indigo orchid—
which of the two I will bring to meet your mother,
the politest way to demur
when she starts to pet my hair.

It fills our hands, this inheritance
that is anything but soft
yet never hard enough to be set
upon a mantle, overlooked.

NO MAN'S LAND

There is a country between us
and it is neither Ghana nor the US.

        It is not the man you haven't fucked yet,

the run of chords
beneath your shorts,
the Langston Hughes
that was our start,
the braid
of sighs flooding
the ankhs
stitched in the fabric
on my wall,
Unathi,
whose father
was shot at the Sharpeville riots,
tugging my twists after her hug
before she looked from you to me back to you
and then down
at the pinstriped floor,
the way you run in the rain,
the Seahawks
sticker on your car,
the page of your back
inside my hands, the
Mariama Bâ letter
I will write when we
are done.

Remember that dog
you lost
to some
speeding train.
The way
I laughed
at how
you mourned.

SPEECH THERAPY

ugly is such a small word,
a stem cell, a tick, a Christmas
package flattened out, static,
almost tragic in a sense, like
a bad smell stuck in skin

famia is much a mauled word,
a Xhosa click, a Shona clap
to those who drawl words,
a five-letter turd of foreign
that is best left untried

baggage is just a tall word,
the Sears Tower, a brunette
nurse with muscular legs,
the kick cheap eggnog has
when you finally put it down

carry is more a sprawled word,
like a name, like a city, like a sex,
female for sure;
a joke I told once, you didn't
laugh or smile or hug me

nigga is quite the droll word
except when it's purring at
the end, when it's reddened,
when it rends, when you mean it,
when you say it like you mean it, said it, say it to me.

it is from my need to matter that I ask you this

you touch me
my pores are pupils
i see you in the crevices of my skin

your knees tickle my eyelashes
your soles *azonto* on an iris
i swipe the tip of my nose
breathing your taste
into my fingers
I cup fireflies as they flicker

                on and off . . .

                    on and off . . .

        do you see this me, more than I could ever be, or the
        me that me and everyone else would see if we only
        took the energy to look hard enough?

. . . that day the earth ripped   gape
like a plum squished in the sun
the rays reflected the thin-veined blood
smeared like grease on the cusp of the sky
the threadbare frays of cumulus clouds
the simper of thunder whispering air into the
mouths of shooting stars

the moon translucent as the dew
gliding
down the underside of a twig

15

the limpid drop
poised
crouched
gone.

the ground split
like a spread-eagled spine
wide as an expanse of belly

did you
bathe
in the
oasis
of my tongue?

FORTY ACRES AND A MULE

The tear in the front pocket
of the suitcase I stole from Timnit
sneers at me. I drag harder. My arm flaps burn.
100 pounds of my life thump down
the splintered stairs. I forgot something.
But I already gave back the key.
The night is indigo marbled gray. The taxi
is a marigold. Rain is needles on my nose,
acupuncture of my failure
to frame this love like art.
The window is a lithograph
of what we were last month,
his chest wet plaster
in my hands,
each eye a different
shade of blue when I melt
butter into his skin.
My toes tangle
in the cloud of carpet,

beige as a
dune in Namibia,

cashew-colored
like our child,

the inside of a tree;

what shame looks like
when you slice it into two.

OUR VERSION OF EVENTS

Your truth
is so important that if you lose it
and you hear a rumor it is hiding
inside your mother's womb and the
only way you can remove
it is with the tip of your penis,
when you do you are innocent
of incest. The word for truth, *nyatepe,* means the

matter's correct
place. This is what
the elders in our father's
village say. You write that your work
is borne from your desire
to tell the stories of the
unseen, to parse the jagged
caverns between our unspoken
and the unspeakable. You say you see
into marrow with that
paintbrush in your hand.
I am editing your essays

for the Columbia MFA.
I shuffle between your bookshelf and
the chair behind your desk, tickling
the piece of tissue kissed by palm oil
with my toes. I am missing some
clothes. The fifth houseboy has
been sacked. I know what swings

between your legs is a catacomb
of tears. In our old house that day

you locked yourself
in the blue guest room,
when you were wearing
what was mine, smearing on musty
lipstick Mummy thought
she'd thrown away, tracing the
name you call yourself over
and over in the mirror, picking
joy out of your teeth with
a vermillion fingernail. We
called for you through the
door, your fingers
turned to talc, unable to peel
off the gown, hide it inside

the spoiled TV, wipe your real
name from the dust, sit in
the Mazda 626, go with us
to the painter's house. You
were certain we had seen
through the concrete to
the cloth. I believed you
when you said Bone
Thugs-N-Harmony were so
dope your Walkman volume
was on max. Now my clothes

are missing. They took ten

19

pounds off my frame.
I know you need them
more than lungs. I will eat
glass to get them back.
How is your life square with a heft
no pain of mine will ever match?
What will the shape of my place be
when you are more daughter than me?

Your truth is a cloud of cotton.
Your truth will crack its shell.
Your truth will kill our father.
You are waiting for him to die.

MAH-MAH

When you left you
took the starch out of
the fufu. I don't
particularly care. I
never really liked
fufu anyway. And so it
won't turn me to salt
that you are never here

                    to pound it.

THE DEVIL IS A LIAR, SAY AMEN?

Religion sounds like
a dirty word.

"Put my religion in your mouth
before your mother
comes home."

Mrs. Osei-Tutu's
voice is clean
as an athlete's sweat.
Her tongue
is habaneros
licking my
back, the cane in her
right hand then
the left, the hate in
rhythm with the glee.
I. will. cast. it. out.
I will cast it out.
Me, Henrietta
Margaret Abena
Asantewaa
Maame Dentah
Osei-Tutu
née Koranteng.
Gargantuan gargoyles
of Satan will not
bloom under my watch!

I will not cry in front of her.
I break in pieces sharp as teeth.
My bladder leaves me on the floor,
the pool of pee shaped like a star.

there are people with cancer
who do not cry this hard

It is not a vacuum cleaner.
It is the machine
that will save my life,
suck out my blood,
part the liquid from
the cells, pour my
essence down the drain,
fill me with something
made by man
that can wick the sick
from my pores.
If I close my eyes
I will stop seeing my father
making a fist each time
he says the word "strong."
If I hold my breath, he will not know
"brave" slides like shampoo
through my hands.
How can I be the clay
that formed beneath his fingers
if I am a pretzel of piss and howls?

THE SWEETNESS OF JUICE

my skin is the color of moonshine mixed with sunshine.
no, it's not. my skin is the color of coal, anthracite,
and black men have died in coal mines too long, showing
their mettle only at the pearly gates (which are white).
Alicia Keys plays the piano, black and white, like her
skin—café au lait, creamy caramel, hazelnut almond,
cocoa vanilla. you never buy aromatherapy called coal.
my skin is dark wood, made for windowsills, never for
windows—transparent, clear, like water, like light—
and black men have tumbled through windows too long,
only to death (which is black). awards are always yellow,
gilded, plantains fry to golden brown. my skin is the
color of soil, earth—my bad—here in America, you call it dirt.
and it's trod on underfoot, breeding trees, bursting forth
like Technicolor. black men have been treated like dirt,
swung from trees, burnt to crisp (which is black) for forty
decades; the color of tar but not feathers—those are light—(so is she).
Veronica is a halo in motion. perhaps the glimpse of Jesus is why you never
notice me.

GAZE

The best
dreams
are the
small ones,
the sort one
sieves with
busy hands.

Novi, those
are the dreams with feet,
the ones
that slink away
without the chore
of having
to come true.

Mine was to come back to school. I thought
I'd go out of my mind, my screams coating
my mother's arms, each limb turned guillotine
with every hug. Both of my parents love
to hug. Guilt woven in my sparking toes,
knowing my tears had fangs friends couldn't see
when they picked up the ringing phone. I cannot
sieve the screaming by which I mean the hugging
which is the writhing, i.e., the drugs, also
the sparking that is the living with roaches
in symbiosis, that is the writing, that is this
truth, that is the noose I made from a belt.
This is a phase; I will get better. I crawled

through islands of salt, I am strong
and I am smart and I'll be fine, and I'll be fine,

and
I'll
be
fine

typing
white
space

after white space.

HOW TO HONOR OUR ILLNESSES

I stick my tongue out. You box my chin.
I hold my breath. You split my lip.
I crack my knuckles. You laugh at me.

There is no honor among thieves. Even less between
a labyrinth and a map. In the tango with my body
we are each both, all the time. My immune system on hibernate,
humming like a radiator with a mockingbird inside, my finger
on the restart button, the power cord inside my throat.

I am still scared
that one day I'll
slit my wrists in my sleep.

I hate myself for being ill,
then wonder if it was perhaps
hating myself that made me ill.

Me and my myelin bite like schoolkids.
There is no referee. No one to stop
me from throwing the first
punch. Begging to be
flattened so the
anticipation ends.

I wring my hands. You pinch my cheeks.

I tear my hair. You kiss my neck.
I gut myself. You stroke my face.

     Tangled here as we are,
     my body, inside each other
     like lesbian hands. You are
     the top. I do not come. You do
     not ask me if I did.

MOSES

I am back home. They say they do not know who I am.
I am as full of angles as a Boer swastika. They say
I was diaphanous. Incandescent. Rubenesque. I have
crawled inside my bones and spun a silkworm's cocoon.

I mumble something about Hogan
and page 172. Not the days I traced out
the map of Ghana with my thumb
rocking back and forth
like a badly mended chair, holding
four simultaneous conversations
in Ewe with myself as I hopped home
on one leg in a torrent of slicing rain.
That time on the bus I followed a woman
all the way to another state
because she looked like someone
who sold groundnuts on our street.
The nights I crunched millipedes
under my heel just to hear
the sound they made
as they ground into the cement
and doodled on a desk, *This*
is the new Middle Passage,
then felt a shame thicker than sap.
I was not kidnapped
or sold. I was banished out of love
so I could be molded
and returned. Now I am back.
Silence snores in every room.

My two degrees
framed on the shelf
smirk in their undulating script.

ACKNOWLEDGMENTS

The poem "it is from my need to matter that I ask you this" was first published as "elixir" on the BN Poetry Prize Shortlist online page.

BLOOD FOR THE BLOOD GOD

MARY-ALICE DANIEL

This is a work of fiction. All names, characters, places, and incidents are a product of the author's imagination. Any resemblance to real events or persons, living or dead, is entirely coincidental.

Published by Akashic Books
©2017 Mary-Alice Daniel

ISBN: 978-1-61775-563-7

Akashic Books
Brooklyn, New York
Twitter: @AkashicBooks
Facebook: AkashicBooks
E-mail: info@akashicbooks.com
Website: www.akashicbooks.com

African Poetry Book Fund
Prairie Schooner
University of Nebraska
110 Andrews Hall
Lincoln, Nebraska 68588

TABLE OF CONTENTS

PREFACE
by Matthew Shenoda

To enter into Mary-Alice Daniel's *Blood for the Blood God* is to embrace a space where time can be suspended or simply conducted in the deeper regions of the imagination, where clocks have no business being. Here it is always night, the past is always present, and there is always a sense of hunger and affliction. We find in her poems a quiet and searing voice intent on reinterpreting the world to create from it a new logic, a logic that seeks, perhaps out of an ultimate desire for healing or redirection, to understand how well humanity has worked to feed the blood god.

Like entering into the interior world of a family album where you see the detailed moments of every member's daily life, the poems show the reader the subtleties and intimate nuances of Daniel's thinking. A thinking reflected in a desire for a new structure, or perhaps a new form of memory; one that takes at its center the earth and its troubling past, the body and its painful earthly struggles.

She challenges the constructs of prevailing logic by commingling its order and breaking apart the notions of clean trajectories:

> you want to tie every desert you've seen to another desert
> you've seen and know water is the same water everywhere.
> *You don't like this coherence:*
>
> (Life is vortex,
> not rotation.)

And it is in that vortex where Daniel's poems take the reader, to a place where there is a desire to pull the world apart in a resistance to rote under-standing and reassemble it as part, of not just a linear continuum, but an un-derstanding of history as a layered dissonance. Daniel's aesthetic inclinations in this vein come out of a growing practice in contemporary African poetry that she is at once responding to and helping to define. The aesthetic arc of her work is shaped from both African and Western poetic traditions, oral and personal memory, theoretical understandings of the world rooted in an unfettered impulse to borrow from these various elements and make something fresh. As she writes in her poem "Disease Map": "You can reduce anything to a set of numbers and elevate any / number to a name."

But Daniel is less interested in this formulaic articulation of the world and instead wishes to rake the territory of human/animal, living/dead, well/diseased, flesh/robotic, to see just how we might find a way forward. As she tells us in her poem "Nightmares": ". . . the body internalizes / the flight-coded language of dreams."

And it is that internalized language, that one that so often suspends time, that she seeks most to cultivate in her work. It is an ethereal language, one that recognizes the whole of the world around us and the world beyond us; the world before us and the world behind us. This vein of thinking comes out of some of the strongest West African histories and traditions of divination, and here Daniel works it into something wholly contemporary and often surprising. There is nothing romantic here, but rather there is a heart in these poems that has given itself to a yearning to feel in a world often mediated by pain and distance, a heart perhaps intent on pumping less blood to the blood god. She continues in the poem "Disease Map":

> A coastline is an unmeasurable thing:
> depending how close you zoom in to how much detail,
>
> twists and turns can extend any boundary infinitely.
> But Baba walked that coast, on leprous legs—
>
> so tired his soul was just dragging its body along on his shoulders,
> *back*

and

back to the ancestry of infection.

Here she reminds us all that, whether conscious of it or not, we are shaped by an antecedent often detailed by multiple diseases, namely the diseases of slavery, conflict, and dispersal, and that we cannot find our way forward without contending with these realities. She also eerily reminds us as we move forward that:

> *The future economy will consist of high-performing*
> *human-computer teams in all aspects of society.*
> We help them along because we now react to emoticons
> the same way we do to the human face.
> ("Wild Ravens that Frolic in Snow Like Children")

And it is perhaps in that very idea of human faces where we find the beautiful resistance embodied in Mary-Alice Daniel's *Blood for the Blood God*, a resistance that seeks to reverse our present reactions and recognize the human face.

INVOCATION

In that sweet voice, Nina Buckless turns on me.
So she says to me, she says to me, she says:

> *I wanna hotwire a red '57 Chevy—*
> *but just to take it around the block*
> *once before returning it where it was . . .*

Tired of delusions, I say: *That's oddly specific.*

We are driving down Main Street in her truck.

It's got 200,000 miles on it   and takes a calamity to turn over.
It is the holiday season, so   the trees dress with pinpricks of yellow light.
They surprise.
They glitter and shatter over us   in a washpoint of starshower.

Nina says: *Careful.*
                Careful what you call down.

I say: *Nina.*
                Nina?
                It isn't like you to caution me.

9

Nina says: . . .

Nina says: *I'm not still Nina, haven't you noticed?*

                                        (So now I am afraid.)

I'm afraid of how her voice turns metallic.
Afraid of how her eyes are painted on.
Afraid of murder as a first resort;
                    extreme cases of the willies;
                            the lack of barrier
                                between *Us*   and *Space*.

Early warning systems
have had a very serious influence
on the formation of my whole heart—

I am afraid of how poems are incantations,
of how my mother used to say:

            Don't whistle out into the dark.
            You will surely call devils here—

                    And what am I doing now but whistling . . .

MUST BE SOME KIND OF SPELL

A boning knife goes missing.
A guest stole something: the mojo
of the home, disturbed. *Your house
isn't haunted—you're just lonely.*

Walking through, after the after-party,
you see chairs arranged in perfect mimicry
of human congregation: assembling in groups

of two or four, dominating space,
facing conversation pieces and food—
                    policing the exits.

And rings of bottles all around the house . . .
And sticky ring stains underneath the bottles
all over my house—

> *concentric cones of hospitality
> radiating out like crop circles.*

They are visual traps.   Also, they are sensory traps.
Also, they are fetishes.   They are effigies.

Objects are animate. They want to return,
like children or brides, to their owners.

The knife was gone.

The mojo of the house disturbed.
The knife turned up

weeks later, when I bent down to fetch a dropped mug:
it was under my bed, in the middle.

No, you must understand—
                                        under the precise center of the bed.

In that spot where children hide
from their parents' punishing arms—

                                                                knife

pointing perfect, straight at my headrest.

BLOOD FOR THE BLOOD GOD

You can do to a body a lot of things.
A feature in *Smithsonian* on cannibals makes me hungry.

I'm learning so much—they use bodies as ritual snacks,
eating everything but teeth, hair, and penis.

(Toenails as pills for stomachache.)

You can view bodies with *aequanimitas*—that clinical practice—
emotional distancing, as of a doctor:

> humans otherwise caught in a net of cable wires,
> humans assimilated into the larger borg.

Or you can want them put down.
Eliminate 350,000 bodies a year to reach optimum population:

If they assume the fetal position,
they can be slaughtered in orderly fashion.

You can make pain principles out of anything: *unripe papaya.*
You can pickle a man in a five-foot-tall glass jar.

Take more men on field trips over battlefields
as melancholy meat: *silhouettes of the national scene.*

You can explain the disappearance of a people by making myth—
say that conquistadors stacked bodies,

then poured cement on top, built them into houses—
thumbed their noses at hauntings and good engineering.

Now zip things in and out of a body
surgically like a Sunday purse.

Wonder how bodies came to be like this . . .
. . . Cannibals use bodies like we all must.

This is the best way, the only natural way:
in anger, in heat. One lonely cannibal,

so upset by his wife's truancy,
twice burned down his own tree house.

BLOODMOON

Our moon should have tipped over
                                into the gulf.

A bad apple falling into a pool,
it was that big and unbalanced.

And so many worlds away—across the Atlantic by coach,
where a bottle of wine makes a good short story.

Past the dead-point of Heathrow, the British Airways lounge
with tesseracting carpet—we pray for God

to lay His Hands on top of the plane,
preventing it from shooting out into the exosphere.

THIGMOTROPIA——*impulse of any *thing* to surround itself:*
                        a thigmotropic roach snug between fridge and wall.
                        The simple audacity in that desire,
                        the plain directive of all life toward comfort.

PSYCHOTROPIA——*incantation that drives you out of your head:*
                        Many ways to cut it,
                        but at the heart,
                        a knife fight.

Combine the two on a darkish coast:
our moon oppressing, overworking waves to spittle.

You are snug—as a bug, as an entire intrusion

15

of roaches slotting into the nasty null of space.

You are an outsider scientist on a shoestring budget,
trawling sky for forests on the moon & the moon towns

dead men sought, back when we still believed in counter-earths.
You can see for yourself
                    that we must be heading Somewhere,

that there must be a force pushing things forward.
With our moon this overripe and present—the world bends.

At this size, our moon blooms.
It cradles; it is orange.

INNOCENT NIGERIANA

Returning to a place after 17 years,
after an uncle's third wife
has bitten the ear off his second wife:

The carpet as the same carpet.
The children are like children.
There is a beehive under the front seat of the Volkswagen.
Dogs Pavlov to another language and what once
               was a house is now a table of water.

A feud that made my mother cry,
and my aunts drive to airport lounges,
calling us in England,
asking what shall they do.

And *road* that should not be called *road*:
more an obstacle than a way through.
We settle in Illela on the cold plateau
where grow custard apples, where
frost kills thirty-five chicks in one night.
    Blue of twilight—only thing
like a body of water we'll see for weeks.

Men pray in the umbrage of a small mountain:
for their wives and their sore throats, for daughters:
girls who belong wholly to their mothers.
At each wedding, a child wears a wedding gown—
the custom of the little bride.

Flies, tenacious as bark, involve themselves

in the work of preparing food.
Mosquitoes pool in the poverty:
swollen plastic bags full of water and bacteria.
Tonight, my arm is a constellation of moonlit bites.

Innocent Nigeriana: the ripe moment.
Engorged world and its quiet. I learn

that goats are afraid of thunder.
The eldest butts its head against
the kitchen door, trying to break in.
The lesser ones bleat pathetically all night,

       wanting to be let inside,
       certain they are human.

VIOLENCE IS MOTHER AND DAUGHTER

There is a superstition that holding a dying creature in adolescence
leaves the offender with trembling hands for life:
perhaps some early violence on my father's part
explains why all the photos of her by his hand are blurred.

The photographs I return to when I feel I could hate my mother:
    —*Memories are white. Ultimately, they are pale snow*—
In here, she scowls in the heat of my uncle's Peugeot 405.

In another, she holds me up to prove
how well she lined my eyes with kohl
to protect them from the desert dryness.
I am a baby with a pink Lamborghini,
selfish with birthday cake.

I wish there were something else—
images more happily complicated,
curled strings and white spaces,
as in her wedding photos.
I am jealous of my father,
having her so young and pretty.

An old boxing ring makes itself a stage,
                    in this one.
      She dances in the spotlight—

                  to music she knows
                  and everyone else knows,
                  but I do not know.

(Her insecurities condensing
a wet hatred for my father and for America.)

Then she is biting her bottom lip, sad.
A box above her: *Orthodynamic Headphones.*
And a framed poem with words I can't make out:

Three lines of *What?*

I grew up this way:
one hand in my mouth and the other
on my mother's breast until I got too old
and she had to fend me off. By ten,
she had broken me.

I used to draw images of her with crayons
in the cleaning closet of the old house,
before they were students,
when we were still refugees.
Between the Domestos thick bleach and the mop,
I drew her hair as a pentagon.

Once I made three lines.
No one could figure out what they were.
Here she appears in a series of green and damaged
concentric circles.

With a paint chipper I hacked fantasies—
she and I would flash in unison, eyes
looking more and more *red* and *rabbit*.
Our world is destroying itself
and all we do is eat, sleep, and groom:

> *Notice attention to detail.*
> *Notice absence of the father.*

FOR MY UNCLE
WHO DIED OF AIDS
CONTRACTED AT THE DENTIST'S OFFICE
(HE HAD A TOOTHACHE)

1. If he dies during the Month of Brides it is a great shame.
2. Wash the body 3 or 5 or 7 times—*Never* 2 or 4 or 6 times.
3. We see Allah rearranging candlesticks in the starry hall of heavens,
   creating spectral shapes, undoing them
   and remixing the music of the situation,
   in widening circles containing us in these compulsions,
   as He wonders which fires He has left unextinguished.
4. Who commits to us these instructions?
   Your heavenly blameless Father,
   His prophets and your earthly fathers:
   superstitions and blind notions.
5. Welcome all to the funeral: Buddhists, followers after Christ,
   those who believe in Chang'e, that lady in the moon
   who sweeps her vast cold palace all alone.
6. Remember the small black dogs your mother dreamt devoured
   each other in play near the incense pit, and know:
   if there are night visions, there are mystical visions.
   There must be a heaven, gods' birthplace—
   therein resides Allah.
7. The face must point toward the House of God in Mecca:
   the living always walk beside or in front of death.
8. Into the grave, place no object!
9. Avoid burial at sunrise, high noon, and sunset.
10. Allow neither music nor emotional outburst,
    for though we surrender our dead to the earth,
    forward from it

    we shall bring them

    once again.

The procedure described above is the only correct one.
To Him do we belong and unto Him is our return.

DISEASE MAP

It's about my aunt getting tuberculosis.
Outbreak in her village is *Devilry* after 1 death, *Risk* at 10.

You can reduce anything to a set of numbers and elevate any
number to a name: *Pandemic* at 100, when the W.H.O. trucks roll in.

Harbingers of infection are chickens, songbirds, or horses.
In TB cases, the first to die are tiny birds learning to sing

the same way children talk—a process of trying and flailing—
in a fucked-up, unbirdlike song.

Otherwise, there's not much warning,
except general wrongness. Hunger and nausea, coupled.

On the disease map,

the wash of pink covering Sokoto State is impolitic:
alluding too obviously to swollen gums.

I believe there are lifetime statistics that should be kept
on all of us: how many times disease has saved your life—

my great-grandfather was captured as a slave
                                                and released.

A coastline is an unmeasurable thing:
depending how close you zoom in to how much detail,

24

twists and turns can extend any boundary infinitely.
But Baba walked that coast, on leprous legs—

so tired his soul was just dragging its body along on his shoulders,
back

and

back to the ancestry of infection.

Lariam (LAH-ree-am)
Generic: Mefloquine hydrochloride

WHAT IS MEFLOQUINE?
Mefloquine is a prescription medication used to prevent and treat malaria.

(It is the drug I take whenever I return to West Africa.)

WHAT ARE ITS SIDE EFFECTS?
Some who take Mefloquine experience sudden, serious mental problems, including:

- anxiety
- paranoia
- hallucinations
- distressing dreams
- disorientation
- unusual thoughts
- unusual behaviors

In some patients, these side effects will continue long after usage is stopped.

WHAT SHOULD I AVOID WHILE TAKING MEFLOQUINE?
Until you know how Mefloquine affects you, avoid using heavy machinery; avoid all activities requiring careful movement. You may lose your balance. Some people who take Mefloquine think about suicide (putting an end to their life). Some people who were taking Mefloquine committed suicide.

WHO SHOULD NOT TAKE MEFLOQUINE?
Do not take Mefloquine if you have had recent mental instabilities, including depression, schizophrenia—or if you have lost touch with reality.

WHAT ELSE?

Do not give Mefloquine to other people, even if they have the same symptoms you have.

It may harm them.

(One woman remained in a Mefloquine-induced psychosis for months.)

HYPERREALITY

1/   We are bound together in a substance called Pan-African Fire.

2/   Butterflies sputter like dying generators.

3/   We pretend we are mercenary to catch mosquitoes.
One we let get away for the emotion most like pity
—(we thought it dying already)—and caught malaria.

4/   The ants so cute with their work ethic,
forming a procession to carry a roach corpse
over the troublesome window ledge.
One looks like panic, circling with a wing bit.

5/   I've heard doors make all kinds of sounds, but this one just giggled at me
                                        &   at night—
                     Operation Avian Moon.

6/   Liquor really starts to become the biggest thing.

7/   Everyone has a personal cloud of bacteria floating around them at all times:

8/   a farcical parade of escalating nonsense

9/   a shocking Sabbath carnival of death

10/ soft shuck of everything on Earth
                         sliding away into space

11/ Here comes trouble from the trouble people.

12/ Animal walking toward those people.

NIGHTMARES

The first thing the dead might say
when they finally get a chance to respond

is: *Sing!*

(Terrible singing—terrible songs.)

The dead may be controversial—they may liken us to birds.
Maybe birds should just go a little wild.

Sometimes the spirit-like quality is pleasing and slight—
but every once in a while I want a little *muscle*—you know?

I don't yet feel the weight of these enormous birds,
because they're only wings and wings are only light.

Parrots do have a presence.
They have the quality of bad visitants—a dire nature in their speech.
Parrots remember your face—(*conspire*)—can find you.

A two-inch feather emerges
from a baby girl's neck:
the body internalizes
the flight-coded language of dreams.

WILD RAVENS THAT FROLIC IN SNOW LIKE CHILDREN

I wake up from a fever dream.
I feel common.

The five most common types of nightmares are:

Tooth falling out   Falling   Public   Naked   Chased

I wake up from a fever dream with a pure directive:
Get a tattoo of the coordinates of the secret gates that free all slaves.
Simple design supersedes action.

[Google "coordinates of the secret gates that free all slaves":
Your search does not match any documents.]

*

Scientists make strides in developing a dream recorder:
The future economy will consist of high-performing
human-computer teams in all aspects of society.
We help them along because we now react to emoticons
the same way we do to the human face.
After implanting chips in volunteers' brains, they find
the subjects can manifest an image, on cue—

Everything Bible-Colored;
Everything in its rightful getting-things-done box;
The Sum of all the various Metaphors for *Body;*
The Location and Extent of an Empire;
The Secret Password of Ravens;

Should Insanity Be Cured?

WHY DOES DREAM LOGIC ALWAYS WORK AGAINST YOU?

That murder may happen.
That murder is the first resort.
That you are anticipated by whatever wants to overwhelm you.
That if the goat-witch in bed beside you climaxes first,
her spells strengthen tenfold.

> *Occasionally you will have only the notion of liking the word* Songster.

An infirm crowd peopling the adult education center,
milling around their widowhood and phobias—
they're in the latter part of animate life.
Inside, they sit so still, so senseless,
the motion-detecting lights turn Off.
One night, a disembodied hand comes through the door,
reaching for the stack of course evaluations.   *Lights On.*
Monks sit still for the camera when they self-immolate: *Lights Off.*

> *Enough Hamletting.*
> In dreams you want grounding. A setting:
> *Let's just pick a cabin where everything runs on fire—*
> *couch, TV, dresser.*

You want to enter the safe space of negative capability:
you want to tie every desert you've seen to another desert
you've seen and know water is the same water everywhere.
You don't like this coherence:

> (Life is vortex,
> not rotation.)

The goat won't either.
She begins speaking in the language of flowers:

vulgar minds.	(marigold, african)
i declare against you.	(belvedere)
i wound to heal.	(sweetbrier)
(pennyroyal):	*flee away.*
(venus's car):	*fly with me.*

Now she has her powers in tens.
Now our private hells grow miniature and masculine:
in terms of risk, the high Antigua forest zone of risk—

> *May flowers throw themselves before your feet*
> *as if the devil is not*
> *and yet*

DISORIENTATION

I'm aware I might not survive this lunar night . . .
I become aware that I might not survive this lunar night . . .

I remember my dreams in the morning like Caedmon:

    Fever was the goat, it said:

              You ate me, Mary-Alice / You wore a boot of me
                        and served the cheese of me to children

I get it—but I was under control—   —Many women have nothing—
I get it—but I wake up

ODD HABITS OF THE MONSTROUSLY LONELY

I wake up from a bad dream and ask if you heard me groaning.
You say no. I try to convince you it should've been that bad.

Those demons coming out of the TV?
Hell mouth. Cracked sequence. Crush on a corpse.
What goes *bump* in the night goes *thump* all day long.

FEEL BETTER

You strap them in a wheelchair crazy as hallelujah
Those amongst us with no impulse control I mean zero

Useless meat puppets   Carnival of bad animals
Show them a picture of eyelash mites no eyelashes seconds later

Chaya in Algeria believed the world would die when the Large Hadron Collider
                                                                rebooted
She thought Earth would crack up and everyone would get pulled like a body
                                                        just getting pulled

Her father tried to divert her attention no such thing
A black hole   That's a bad end
The television is irresponsible saying eclipse is omen

The rabble rushes to temple ignoring scientists warning nothing to fear calm
                                                yourselves calm calm
No wonder humans are called long pigs   Not only for taste

Chaya ran from the evening news straight to the bleach you've already guessed
                                                she chugged it
That isn't cosmic that's belly pain that's human
Goodbye to your mother with chlorine on your breath

Hallelujah is the wrong word to begin with so start over
Tiny tiny crazy baby steps toward mass compulsion

SOURCES REFERENCED

http://www.smithsonianmag.com/ist/?next=/travel/sleeping-with-cannibals-128958913

"Nodus Tollens"—www.dictionaryofobscuresorrows.com/post/48395591256/nodus-tollens

Mefloquine Label FDA.gov

http://www.cnn.com/2014/01/27/world/asia/china-jade-rabbit-moon-rover-goodnight/

http://www.cracked.com/blog/5-sci-fi-dystopias-weve-actually-created-for-animals/

http://www.theguardian.com/books/2013/oct/19/david-birnbaum-jeweller-philosopher

http://lifecoachforprofit.com/blog/2016/04/13/29-insanely-elaborate-custom-coffins-from-ghana/

http://www.realclear.com/offbeat/2016/02/24/three_youtube_mysteries__12913.html

ACKNOWLEDGMENTS

The following poems have appeared or are forthcoming in these publications:

"For My Uncle . . ." *Callaloo*: forthcoming.

"Nightmares," *Hysteria Anthology*. Lucky Bastard Press: forthcoming. Also, *Hayden's Ferry Review*: Issue 56 (Spring/Summer 2015).

"Blood for the Blood God," *Cutthroat Journal*: forthcoming.

"Violence is Mother and Daughter," *Painted Bride Quarterly*: Issue 92, November 23, 2015. Online.

"Must Be Some Kind of Spell," *Wide Awake: Poets of Los Angeles and Beyond*. Pacific Coast Poetry Series: March 2015.

"Feel Better," *American Poetry Review*. November 2014: Volume 43, No. 6.

"Disease Map," "Bloodmoon," "Hyperreality," *Nimrod International Journal of Prose and Poetry*: Volume 58, Number 1 (Winter 2014).

"Invocation," "Why Does Dream Logic Always Works Against You?" *Waxwing*: October 2014.

"Must Be Some Kind of Spell," *Anti-*: Issue 14, May 26, 2014. Online.

i know how to
fix myself

ASHLEY MAKUE

Published by Akashic Books
©2017 Ashley Makue

ISBN: 978-1-61775-569-9

Akashic Books
Brooklyn, New York
Twitter: @AkashicBooks
Facebook: AkashicBooks
E-mail: info@akashicbooks.com
Website: www.akashicbooks.com

African Poetry Book Fund
Prairie Schooner
University of Nebraska
110 Andrews Hall
Lincoln, Nebraska 68588

Table of Contents

Preface: Praise and Fire

by Honorée Fanonne Jeffers

It is no hyperbole to say that women can never free themselves of their mothers. The familiar way the knees might knock together or how the hips might spread, an arc reaching back through generations. The voices of mother and daughter, the sound of their breaths leaving their body, might even hiss identical. And many times, emotional—painful—longings get passed down through female heredity in what South African writer Elaine Vera has called "writing near the bone." The tearing of flesh unleashes the past, along with the stories of trouble and tides.

We see the writing of ancestry, the pain of it, in the chapbook of Vera's countrywoman Ashley Makue, *i know how to fix myself.* The title of this cluster of powerful, devastating poems implies there's a flaw in the poet that needs repairing, and that flaw is ancestry. The speaker in the very first piece offers an ancestral litany: "my great-great-grandfather begets my great-grandmother. my great-grandfather begets my grandmother. My grandfather begets my mother. my father begets a ghost." The last word of this poem implies a haunting: the speaker will never be free. And the strangeness in this piece that opens up Makue's world—or her speaker's world, if one insists on critical distance—is that men beget the women. The act of making a masculine enterprise, a patriarchal, patrilineal undertaking. And what the men beget is flesh through sowing and pain through love's devastation. And these men are never sorry.

Makue's is a lyric biography, a daughter's witness to the world of men and women. And at first, she is the child who sees all. Each poem is written in lowercase, which may simply be a stylistic choice, as with the poems by the American writer Lucille Clifton. But when viewed on the page, the eschewing of capital letters appears metaphorical, an indication that the poems' main "character" continues to evolve. Though angry, though hurting, she is confident that she possesses the agency to complete her repair. She doesn't *hope* she can heal herself. She "knows how to fix" herself.

And there is much mending needed, for the woman who gave birth to her—"mom"—is extraordinarily wounded. The first few poems focus on a mother who is crumbling and cannot rebuild her foundation. This is the woman who gave birth to the poet. Her wounds have been made by men, ruthless in their actions, and all the more so because they pretend to be kind. But if it's true that making is a masculine act—whether the making of children or the making of anguish—then *who* is making these poems? Is the author still alive? Is what follows written/told from the afterlife? No, the poems are told from this earthly place, but by a woman who initially decorates corners with her shadows. She has not yet emerged.

Makue's first six poems address ancestry, but by the time we reach the second half of the chapbook, the poet—the speaker—takes over. The different pronouns—*I, you, we*—are conflated. The speaker of the final eight poems is a personal figure, but she stands for a group of women who are her forebears. She is their appointed memory. These final poems are communal lyrics that establish both individual confidence and collective, female survival. And they are calm (though never dispassionate) pronouncements of what the poet repudiates and what the other women of her (now) matrilineage have rejected as well.

Ancestry continues to be important. This is an honest gathering, and no woman can be left behind, for female kin are a particularly sacred link. But something has changed. Men no longer hold onto the leathered extensions of power. And in the title of the penultimate poem, "my aunt on leaving her husband of twenty years," Makue signals to us that an extraordinary act by an everyday woman has taken place. With this act, the patriarchy and the patrilineal—the tracing of women's lives through men who control them—are over, at least for the chronicler/speaker of this chapbook. This woman (whom we assume to be of Makue's line, if not the poet herself) will no longer be made by a man; thus, women will be the agents of their own change, and also their own pain, for better or worse. And this bravery, this capstone of utterance, is the demonstration of Makue's great gift.

i know how to fix myself

my great-great-grandfather begets my great-grandmother. my great-grandfather begets my grandmother. my grandfather begets my mother. my father begets a ghost.

seasons of alone

the winter scatters the strands
of your hair like cluttered echoes
like chasing your father uphill
like a purse as unkempt as your mother's heart

your mother was a spring day when she had you
and then the dust
and the wind
and the things that are torn away

in the summer
you wear your father's broad shoulders
like a new christmas day two-piece
or your father's things wear you

fruits don't ripen in the autumn
or you losing your grasp on a branch
falling not too far from your mother
from hollow

from lonely

a clutter of things

oh wrecked soul
how dirty the things
that you find to hog
the torture will not end
neither will the conflict heal
but what peace should there be
in a city where rocks
toss people

mom goes

grandma calls prayer meetings
and we sing around fire in the night
wind prancing about fire
mistake
danger

that is where i learned to love like carcass
and yelling that i have been cheated
like open mines are not earthquakes in the night
tragedy
accident

in grandmother's shoes
mom stands shorter than she is
in mom's own shoes
she is traveling away

question
mom leaves or mom disappears
answer
mom goes and grandmother's
daughter remains behind mom's shell

i think i like it here
but i don't know how to stay
mom goes
thievery

they say that love is not supposed to hurt

i think they mean that god didn't get angry
and drown our body
cause
effect

mom's shoes are flooded
in them i cannot swim up to breathe
i think it means that i am bad for you
accident
something bad has happened

my sister plays house
drags my shoes around the house
she's in the eye
i cannot pull her out
and be the hurricane at the same time
disaster

mom's on fire

she says two prayers every night
one for herself and one for him
she prays that her clitoris rots
and that his penis disappears

she cries as she floods the bathtub
in the bathwater
she is a sunken dream
her triggers set against herself

my mother is a war zone
they don't tell her that
these men that pee in her
and leave with gunpowder in their chests

i hear my mother's bones shatter
from her bathroom floor
i hear him shout that she started the fire
i hear her cry his name like blasphemy

her face keeps the jabs
the fistfuls of contempt
my mother brings men to their knees
and they split her open

she calls men to themselves
beasts incognito playing "nice gentlemen"
with her they are bare
they hate this about her

i ask her one day
what is the point
of setting yourself on fire
to see how quickly the devil catches the flame

mom's language on fire

in my mother's language
fire also means zeal

my father lit a storm
in my mother's womb
and she gave birth
to a ball of fire

this whole time
i have been screaming
and wailing
for sand

in my mother's language
land also means sovereignty

to a paranoid people
smoke without fire
is witchcraft
and running and running

put me off i am
on fire
put sand over me
i am burning

sounds like a praise
song

this whole time
i have been rolling
on sand
burning

burning sand
is no one's sovereignty
i have not been fierce
i have been on fire

in my mother's language
quiet also means dead

i have only known quiet men
and men who left widows
i could never tell
if my grandfather was still or dead

i am told that my father
was dead before he was buried
quiet fathers do not say anything
when their daughters are on fire

in my mother's language
father also means man

we learn early
that calling a man
your father might make him come
but it will not cause him to stay

i have been calling men father
my whole life
a quiet man
is no one's father

in my mother's language
soul also means wind

the wind is on fire
my soul is burning
my mother is a dried-up river
the quiet man is not my father

my soul is on fire
the wind blew flames here
my mother has no water
the quiet man is not my father

in my mother's country
water is symbolic of life

there will come men
knocking at my grandmother's door
asking for a cup of water
my body is on fire

they offered him my hand
and watched him leave
hands intertwined
with a volcano

in my mother's language
walking also means leaving

my mother has been leaving
since she was two
a late bloomer
soon she will walk and not come back

corroded

we the rusty ones
we the rowdy ones
crinkle and fracture
old bones when we walk
rubble when we exhale
find our mothers in the debris
uncle hands up our young thighs
what's youth
so many suns past
our fathers behind the moon
no marrow
just sewage
comatose torsos
what's worth saving
lethargic fingers
puncture when touched
what's to tell
there's nothing to see here

explosive

love stirs you up all wrong
that is not supposed to happen

why didn't you swallow the roses dark one
pour your vaginal fluids in a cup
and drink them until you're a spring day

you have got to shed your skin now baby
it's not pretty to wear your father's sins like that

that's not how you fall in love
you don't make friends out of strangers
you don't show them all that is written on your body

your eyes are pocket knives
you are just like your mother

heart swimming in the whale

she's a double-edged sword
with a tongue covered in scripture
she potters you like clay
coaxes your army's guard down
she knows how to make you
love her until you hate yourself
you are jonah in the whale's mouth
she carries you to deep water
before she throws you up
love is deep water
at the deep end
you beg the whale to swallow you again

absent

i don't know what it is
about leaving
and unavailable
and out of reach
and someone else's
and begging
and desperate
and alone
and torturous
that lures me to you
i know that you're not mine
i think that's the thing

i am sorry
that i will lie
and build a home around you
i am sorry
that i will swallow you
and keep you in
at the cost of all my breath
i am sorry
that i will not blink
i will not move
i am sorry
that you cannot trust
me
i am sorry
that i will ask you to

i don't know what it is
about fighting to lose
about fighting and losing
and burning
and fire
and waves
crashing into a body
sleeping with corpses
being dead
and wanting you
for as long
as you don't want me
you don't want me
i think that's the thing

everything ages

i like new things
i smell like smoke
and
spilled milk
i should've kissed your knuckles
i should've been kinder

i like the taste of gasoline
hearing my chest collapse
i like infinity
i shouldn't have waited up
i have no use for memory

i wish new days
broke out of nowhere
pure from midnight
from yesterday's residue
i keep asking you to stay

i don't know how to keep you
i smell like seawater
like drowning
sickness
i cannot stay

for tebogo: the exercise to becoming our mothers

the breathalyzer

my best friend knows how to
catch a boy's breath
and hold it
until it's filled with her name
she knows how to hold his gaze
until she's a mental note

the eye test

you cannot keep two words in a mouth
keeping his name pushes yours out
what is in a name
you are not a rose
if he calls you colorless
this is why your father left

the urine sample

there are casualties in every war
even when you're fighting alone
everything you do is an apology
you give more than you should
so that you should apologize
you're sorry you're just like your mother

23

the paternity test

missing your father is how you become your mother
the liquor and drunkenness
all of the things it claims
fathers who leave
should pack the shame with them
and the sitting on mattresses

the maternity test

you are still holding the boy's breath

my aunt on leaving her husband
of twenty years

that day i felt the flood
in my chest
come too close to the throat
i felt the years of drifting
of water
of drowning

yes
i knew i couldn't swim
when i made love in the river
in murky water
your uncle is dirty
an ulcer
i let grow too close to my heart
maybe that's why he did it
because i begged him to

when i chose him
i chose the touch of glass
the swallowing of timeworn blood
the eating of mold

so i have daddy issues
although i don't know the science
of having daddy issues when
you don't have a daddy
but i know loss
i know my husband's tight hold on my neck

and me jizzing my panties
i know him throwing me to a wall
and me wanting to pop
my pussy for him
i know loss
i know my father's country denying me entry
i know my body as betrayal
your uncle is a pill
i should have swallowed him with holy water

i was sick
but i didn't take medication
he wasn't sick
but he was on the drug
made him sick
made me crazy
made him sick

i left him because i dreamed of fire
my mother said that
you are everyone in your dreams
i didn't want to be the fire burning me
i left him when the paint
fell off the cracks

your uncle is an explosive
i don't know what that makes me
wrapping my legs around
a threat
for twenty years
he didn't know how to steal

until i showed him how to steal from me

i have mother issues
my mother has mother issues
my grandmother had mother issues
i put sand over my daughter
so that i wouldn't drown her accidentally
i don't like accidents

your uncle was not a mistake
the twenty years of holding a gun to my head
and putting it away
and letting him suck my nipples
and putting him away
and letting him inside
and calling dibs on the injury
that was on purpose

your uncle is a hatchet
i buried in my crotch
on purpose

eventually you breathe
on purpose

peace offering

i have decided that
love may no longer
summon me to war
i have laid off my troops
blood-bathed my body
clean of all sin
i will no longer kiss
like breaking my law
or make love
like being broken into
i will clear my eyes
of all my specks
and then i shall see you

you see
these are the days
of the sweet treaty

THE BOOK OF GOD
EJIOFOR UGWU

This is a work of fiction. All names, characters, places, and incidents are a product of the author's imagination. Any resemblance to real events or persons, living or dead, is entirely coincidental.

Published by Akashic Books
©2017 Ejiọfọr Ugwu

ISBN: 978-1-61775-565-1

Akashic Books
Brooklyn, New York
Twitter: @AkashicBooks
Facebook: AkashicBooks
E-mail: info@akashicbooks.com
Website: www.akashicbooks.com

African Poetry Book Fund
Prairie Schooner
University of Nebraska
110 Andrews Hall
Lincoln, Nebraska 68588

TABLE OF CONTENTS

PREFACE
by Patricia Jabbeh Wesley

Ejiọfọr Ugwu's chapbook, *The Book of God,* offers a fascinating treatment of the African sensibility. Deeply rooted in Nigerian mythology, oral tradition, and religion, *The Book of God* could have well been written by someone from an earlier generation of African poets who explored African oral traditional images with that keen sense of freshness and authenticity, untarnished by today's new diasporic and global experience. Ugwu's penetrating images call to mind great poets like Christopher Okigbo or Kofi Awoonor, whose powerful poetry nurtured the younger generation of African poets who were born or came of age during the beginning of Africa's independence from colonialism. Here, we are seeing a twenty-first-century rebirth of our literary forefathers.

The book is authentically African while remaining universally powerful in its exploration of life and death, the belief in sacred shrines and gods, engaging both the ancestral world and the world of the living in conversation, bridging the gulf that separates the living from the dead, and forcing us into dialogue with the dead. *The Book of God* is a celebration of African oral tradition, the religious connection to our ancestral spirits or the indictment of ancestral shrines and ghosts as a Nigerian motif to explore our experience as a people.

The speaker draws upon African mythology and traditional religious belief that the dead are not really dead, and that the world of our ancestors occupies a place in the world of the living. In many ways Ugwu's poems do not have to struggle to help us see this reality but simply bring to us a world that we already know or should know, where the spirits of the dead exist alongside the living even as the living seek to know their dead loved ones, to bring them back into conversation. In "The Buried Dead," the speaker says:

I opened my father's grave today
in search of his bones
and mother's long-gone love;
such that a love buried in
a makeshift wood box could still
be recovered after a decade of . . .
I set out to reclaim this prized love for
my mother.

Scattered throughout the book are images of the dead, the dying, and the decayed, people who just die without being ill, but in their dying, they continue to be a part of the living world, either tormenting this world as ghosts or refusing to go away despite the attempt to bury them. Even while the living are dying or die without being ill, worms from their rotten dead bodies continue to live on or leave behind only small bones that remain in the father's grave, and in the midst of all of this, there is the silence.

In "The Buried Dead," the speaker can open his father's grave in search of bones. In "Children of the Moon" we can "dip our souls / for the rite of ukpara." In this world of African oral tradition and religion, there is no demarcation between the world of the living and the world of the dead, and there is that constant struggle between the world of the ancestors and the world of the living to coexist. Ugwu's speakers are constantly seeking to bridge the divide, to understand both the world of the living and of the dead who are not really dead.

The title poem, "The Book of God," is one of the most powerful works in the chapbook. In six parts, it is an autobiographical exploration of the speaker's relationship with his already-dead father. It tells the story of the father's book of God, kept in a sacred place in a large extended family. The father's book of God chronicles all of the birth dates, the dates of the death of family members, and many other important incidents in the family. It is also the storehouse of old receipts, invitation cards to weddings, bills from the father's bar life, as well as the "Sacramentals / and dates of completed confessions." But even in "The Book of God," the speaker reminds us of the dead and the dying. Memories and images of death fill this poem too, and it seems the only constant in the Ugwu's own *Book of God* are ghosts, ancestral spirits, the dying, and the dead.

The clapbook is filled with "half-woken stars" and "broken moonlights." And there is another interesting image running through the book, that of the "mother," who stands firmly in the world of the living among all the rest who have died or are dying. She is life, love, and hope in a book where death represents more than death itself. Mother is the reason for hope, the link to the family line, the one with news of the dying, the one who seems to redeem the runaway son.

Ugwu's poems are filled with biting images of pain, decay, rot, and a satirical depiction of a society that is so corrupt that the living find themselves visited by dead ghosts and spirits of the dead. As if the living need the dead to keep them alive and the dead to keep the living dead, images of death overtake the book. This is a collection that uses death as a symbol of loss and destruction to portray how corrupt the world of the living has become. This is not a book that is dark or that depresses. Instead, Ejiọfọr Ugwu's *The Book of God* is an honest and powerful examination of the intricate relationship between the living and the dead, a book deeply rooted in our African oral tradition and mythology, an urgently necessary book that takes us back to our roots.

RATS

When you sleep in the midst of rats
a night so beautifully started
can be un-night,
then you keep sleepwalking
on rat tracks,
the feces forming slippery pads.
Rats are very movable people.
They sleep very little at night.
Rats don't sleep at night.
And it happens to you that
the man next door
escaped the war of rats
when he took sleeping pills
and woke up in his silent coffin,
chewing away at his own lips,
crying out blood.
Life cleans up the world that way.
But why do men keep rats
in their inner rooms?
And for the last time, the voice spoke:
It's a rat world.
You only live to keep them out
or on the way.
They like human flesh.
They are carnivores, always busy
sharpening their claws and incisors.

THE BURIED DEAD

I opened my father's grave today
in search of his bones
and mother's long-gone love;
such that a love buried in
a makeshift wood box could still
be recovered after a decade of
making familiar the loneliness of
graveworms and fetishizing absence.
I set out to reclaim this prized love for
my mother.
Those now frequenting
our housefront with snuff bottles
and murmurings of kinship do not care
whether there were once
bones of earnest desires.
They have come to help mother bury him
so that he will now be dead.
I moved in, instead,
daring ghosts and foul air and dumb foretellers dressed in remote gowns,
killing the dawn at the cemetery.
I worked on the mound, upturning everything that
has been keeping him deep down and mute since a decade or so ago.
I saw that the bones are gone,
except for the little-sized ones, fully dressed up
for what looked like a banquet.
They looked away
in a cruel moment of silence,
and for me, shock. They sized the way to
their journey and departed,

leaving only me and the famished termites behind;
the humming hunger almost
making me lose the sand under my feet.
I am going home
to meet Mother with absence
and silences,
and muddy sand;
I am carrying the hunger of the graveworms
with me, and their love.

CHILDREN OF THE MOON

I come from the tribe
of Circles—
bridging the lions' roars
in our ancestral shrines
the waters gush in pulsated rhythms
into the potted holes
beside the seats of our gods
from where we dip our souls
for the rite of ukpara
when rotten by blood
or lies from distant holies
we commune with the moon
in filaments,
knitting fragments
emptying into corals of egbachukwu,
and we hear birthsongs
in akparata traveling
through the soft mutters of sand:
we too are the ancestors.

Endnotes
*ukpara—a rite of cleansing.
*egbachukwu—an annual feast of God.
*akparata—native coffins.

SUNRISE

The sun was reluctant to rise,
holding grudges
from the dead night.
The gloom spread,
catching up with all of us.
I scooped water
from the mud pot
to rinse my face
and help the sun rise
and speak our cause.
I fear my demons too.
They keep erupting
everywhere.
Even in my dreams,
I see whiteness
and blinding lights.
The angels came.
They see decays,
we see dancers.
My dreams are diseased.
My dreams grow moths.
The rope almost loops
in an obvious feast of beheading.

MAGUN

He locked her clitoris
with a silver pad
and threw the key
into the sea.
But I am a sea child:
I untied my boat
from the water bank,
the rope snapped,
I looked away.
I am bound with, bound
to the sea.
I am a sea child.
I armpitted my paddle,
my boat on my head,
and set out for the sea under.
What is it with me and
the life of swamps?
What is it with me and
the foundations,
the concealers,
the pressed powders,
and the nude shades of
shadow?
I am made that way.
I am a sea child,
Sea children are
children of tides.
Then she began to decay,
her flesh too young

for the rust of silver.
She is from the ancestry
of wood demons
unknown to him.
He has locked
my penis, too,
I, too, decayed
in the cold of
the lower sea
but I am a sea child.
I know the
smell of the sea.
I grew up in the
underwater stones.
No one knows my name.
My own clumps of
seaweed are
for the beasts alone.
I will surely return
before dusk.

ASHFIELD

This asphalt, fresh from the ashfield, has
no kith and kin with men in want of culture,
no love, none of the kind for men.
The lined flowers moisten the
tarmac, the sidewalk flowers reddened by menstrual blood,
the spit of
metropolitan fumes, fresh from
the mill.
Today is the feast of the unleavened bread.
A dog, the color of mountain,
chain on the neck, lapping up stray spit,
staggering legs, bald fur, limps in
the middle of the funeral home
Wild doves watch over the nights,
marking times with every coo,
waking up sentinels in long-distant dreams.
They announce the call of the blood,
the blood of the dog on the tar, close to
the home for the entombed beasts,
the mad healers ready in the madhouse.
They tend the order of the fallen world,
most, words, uttered to dead pillows.
Vultures beak to death the straying flies perching on its neck,
the chain coming off, setting the worms free, for the first time
dark is the color of burnt coal and
frozen tobacco.
The song on the restless tar
has been the munching of stones,
goose egg stones and chippings
naming names that only the graves can bear.

THE PLAGUE

for Kofi Awoonor

And they hurried him away
into emptiness,
and so will his blood
gather fire,
and the millions still blazing out
all over the Sahara.
I am curled up here in Ajaokuta
atop a rock
where the sun has gone to bed,
my chin heavy in my hands
waiting,
watching
as the blood pursues us and
the diseased earth
till the world is eaten away
so that we can live.
There is life in our dust.

LORES AT THE SHRINE

Strands of shawls
and palls in colors of a dying sun,
dark, gray and red—
we heard mutterings
from the fount of ghosts;
lines of bloodied feathers
and shells of sea lives
snaked and twisted through
the heart of the Deep
till the Votaryhead
breathed the air of
the singing virgins,
witches and wizards,
of sacred emissaries
in clatters of thunder.
Ebọgidịgidị uncoiled
in a log of python
smeared in corals of deep sea vents
and bathed
in the waters
and listened.
"We have never refused a call!"
I heard the leader of the wizards.
I had come for rebirth in
the mid of the starless night.
The fire from the snakestools
struck smokeclouds into
my eyes and I lost count of
the strange inhabitants

and familiar voices,
faces of my day life and nightdreams,
faces of our marketplaces
and faces of village guilts,
faces of war deaths from
my father's civil war stories,
those gone for the peace of
afterwar life, and its curse,
like the victims of Ndi Sehven
killing to secure their
personal happinesses,
people for whom the war was booties.
The faces turned into dustclouds and
settled under the stools,
making owls fight over
worms among the dust
the witches from the distant within
chattered in their tuberous laps behind
the clouds.
And I sensed an unbelonging.
Binaries of beads
splashed fires again before
the feet of the gods
and our eyes clamped.
"My son, you will come back!"
And I heard a voice in the form of
a consoling mother.
A stream guzzled behind me
and I followed the peels of the flute.
I was still fanning the logfire
and mother's night food

was eating deep into the dark.
My rebirth will come
I hoped—
a feast of my true coming.

THE ROAD

There will be less men in
my village by the time I
return to it again.
Yesterday, Dona died.
I was happy.
He gave me lashes
for having my own class most times
under that mango tree
close to the village shrine.
Today, Mother called.
Mosi had died of thin disease.
And the other day again,
Owom fell from a tree.
Again, on the day before Palm Sunday
Nwezem died.
He was a man of many books.
A day before the other day
Father died.
I got my things and left.
What do you miss when you
leave the land of the dead?
You miss stray muds,
stuttered steps,
grandma's hollow eyeballs,
frail shrinehouses,
decaying Gods,
empty farms,
dry rivers,
arid thatch mountains,

drunken youth,
and those already set
for journeys
farther than their eyes can go.

THE BOOK OF GOD

I

When the time came
in that small world of
half-woken stars
and broken moonlights
we were gathering palmnuts,
uncracked palmkernels of
previous years
lying silent in the dust
breeding thick, and lice
termites eating away detachable peelings
and building endless houses,
eating up sand.
I was a boy of unspecified age.
It must have been the time
we took ogwu uwa—the drug that
cured the whole world.
I don't remember.
My father knew everything for us.

II

He wrote all—
our memory—in
his St. Martin's de Porres prayer book, half-eaten
by worms: birth dates,
the date of his father's death,
and that of his mother (she died of
water disease, or so, his footnote),
dates of lands leased out
and the leaseholders' names
and the reasons for the lease
like the return of dowries
when his sister divorced
a barren husband of many years;
the date he buried her too
(she died of madness or
adultery or so).
The leaves of the Book of God
are also interspaced with
receipts of old sales,
weatherbeaten complimentary cards
with long-distant dates,
wedding invitation cards,
receipts of beer bars,
guest house lodgings
and stopover names,
receipts of Sacramentals and
dates of completed Confessions
(baptismal cards
or dates of child dedications? No),

sketches of unknown animals,
or was that a skeleton of an owl?
or naked bats?

III

He hid the Book of God
in an iron box that day
he saw me watching the portrait of
the saint. St. Porres looked like
someone in pain, angry, helpless, the flesh on
his face folded into indistinct shapes,
like a mother weeping an only son.
At this time, father no longer smiled.
He ate his teeth so often
and climbed
his woodbed every night reeking of gin.
He died later, gathering all his
old music tapes at the head of his bed,
his candle Rosary on his neck.

IV

I don't remember,
my father was memory.
Or was it the time we
used to run about naked in the village,
playing hide-and-seek,
or when we used to bathe in the streams
and sometimes hide away the
clothes of bathing women?
I don't remember.
I only remember wet
soaking up the raffia mat, and
our urinating on soldier ants
in the daytime could not help
as Mama Nnukwu would instruct (they
refused to come for us in the nights
and we wetted the dreams as if it was daylight).
Our clothes:
mine a jumper and shorts
with a pair of round holes at
the bottom.

V

We would wake up in
the midnight, run
to the fireside,
sit on the fire,
burn the liquids,
gather smokesclouds and
smells of fire,
enter the cloth blanket again
and feel warm.
I lay head down
Kachi's head facing Mama's side,
her legs overtaking my head.
She was a grown woman
and I would rise, as I always did,
and she would fall.
We burrowed aimlessly into
each other's mid-regions,
the big mother snoring
away her peace in her bamboo bed.
Sometimes she would wake,
stand on us,
calling Kachi, waking her to
stop talking in her dreams:
we were awake as rats under the cloth.

VI

Kachi's mother has been
seeing the Mother of Christ in
front of the village chapel,
close to the church cemetery since
She left;
and that was after she said to me
after many years of getting lost in the world:
"Owom, you are now a big boy,"
and we shared a smile.
In that palmkernel house of my grandmother,
we used to gather straying nuts
in an unpaid labor; we
gathered them to make heaps of fun.
we played on the heaps—me, Kachi, and others—
then we destroyed them at
the next cock crow.
Kachi left without confessing
our sins on the heaps of lice sands,
she died of no disease,
she just died.
Last night she came in
my dream and gave me her mouth.
I now speak in the name of the dead.

ACKNOWLEDGMENTS

Thank you to the editors of the following publications in which these poems have appeared:

Guernica: "Rats" and "Sunrise"
The Kalahari Review: "Lores at the Shrine"
Drumtide Magazine: "Children of the Moon"
Cordite Poetry Review: "The Book of God"
Elsewhere Lit's African poetry anthology: "The Buried Dead"

TAKE ME BACK
CHEKWUBE O. DANLADI

Published by Akashic Books
©2017 Chekwube O. Danladi

ISBN: 978-1-61775-572-9

Akashic Books
Brooklyn, New York
Twitter: @AkashicBooks
Facebook: AkashicBooks
E-mail: info@akashicbooks.com
Website: www.akashicbooks.com

African Poetry Book Fund
Prairie Schooner
University of Nebraska
110 Andrews Hall
Lincoln, Nebraska 68588

TABLE OF CONTENTS

> *Strange, my dear, these your eyes, they swallow everything.*
>
> "Oji Lake Police College"

Nigerian-born Chekwube O. Danladi is, simply put, one of the truly excit-
ing poets emerging today. I am already hungry to read a full collection of
her poems, and especially keen to read her *fifth* collection, which, no doubt,
will be heralded as "the anxiously anticipated new work of one of our true
legislators of the human experience." It is fair to recognize the whimsy of
hyperbole here, but I have imagined her future writing in light of the surety
of continued work that this splendid chapbook collection, *Take Me Back*,
represents.

Danladi's work offers that hard-to-achieve combination of lyric engage-
ment with the self—psychologically vulnerable and filled with risk—and a
deeply committed and daring exploration of the complexity of politics. In
poems like "Say My Name," "The Earth's Own Abomination," "Qui Parle,"
and "When I First Encountered Kwame Nkrumah's Crypt, I Laughed," we
understand that she is exercised by the current politics of war and violence
around the world, as it pertains to Africans and people of African decent.
And in all of this, she is constantly alive to the poetry that has come before
her and the work that is happening around her. She invokes Chris Abani,
Kofi Awoonor, and Chinua Achebe in poems that show no slavish homage
but continue a conversation fully aware of what she owes and where she
must take her own poetry. There is in her a roving intelligence, an exciting
sense that language is filled with traps and possibilities, especially when she
is negotiating her lost Ibo and Hausa tongues and her consuming English,
and even as she is moving through various landscapes. Ultimately, her poems
are anchored by the voice of her "aunt," a woman who constantly feeds us
with wisdom and a poet's sense of the world.

The shifts from the personal, in which Danladi explores the history of blood clots and fibroids, to the public collective tragedies of African history—such as the work of King Leopold II that she describes in "Leopold II Defends His Philanthropy Under Le Association International Africaine"—are a consistent strength of this collection. The language retains the sense of what a body can do even as Danladi manages to write what is largely a celebration of the body as a site of pleasure, and disturbingly, a lament for the body as a site of abuse and torture.

Danladi, in so many of her poems, demonstrates her uncanny ability to use the finely observed details that we associate with realism to, by the distortion of magnification, turn them into something quite surreal and disruptive. The effect is a heightened realism, and when applied to the details of a relationship between two people finding themselves in a place of rupture or prerupture, the effect is emotionally and intellectually compelling: "We'll both seek sex after. / I'll turn my back to you, / you'll teeth the flesh of my neck, / offer my belly the embrace of a cold hand" ("Arpeggio").

At the heart of Danladi's defiant optimism is the sensuality of the body and something she later refers to as the "Phenomenology of Excess." There is, in "Communion" for instance, a willful profusion of metaphors, similes, allusions to the intense abundance of the senses that declares, "I am never abandoned." There is always food, there is always the fecundity of the body, and there is the sexual democracy of desire for the "praise of generosity" she sees in men who "leak star milk into their laps" and women "who have spread [her] sweet, / called [her] tangelo." The secret to all of this is that at the end of the day, the imagination is happily wanton, and the poems reflect this wonderful energy.

But this is an energy that the poet's body draws from others, especially those she recognizes as part of her legacy and the making of self, like Mma (her mother) in "Pull the Chord," whose wounds she promises to wear someday. There is also the mother who seems to have her own life—a life independent of children, a life in another country that we see explored in

6

"Say My Name," in which this tantalizing passage appears of her mother in England: "In Manchester, my mother considers gestation, / naming children in the cold."

It is irrelevant whether this is the same mother we have met earlier in the collection. Danladi's mothers are splendidly varied and complex even as they haunt her imagination. Her mother does become a nurturer, a figure who stands as a source of protection and constancy, and part of a deep connection to Nigeria, a place of primal and urgent memory for Danladi that comes to her in smells and tastes and colors. In a parents' nightmare of a poem, "Tomorrow, Chaka Demus Will Play," the speaker remains tethered to her mother, who is at home sleeping and seemingly oblivious to the daughter's sneaking out at night with a miniskirt in her purse, to go dancing, to allow herself the sensuality of drink and desire of this new country, only to return to the home space of jollof rice and coffee "to mask the lust / oozing from [her]," and a sleeping mother. But her mother is also part of the legacy she carries in her body, whether it is in her skin or the shape of her breasts or in the fibroids she finds in her, causing her to wryly declare, "Tell me something of history."

Other women populate her world, too, some in passing, like the woman in the closet at a party ("Phenomenology of Excess") who laughs while wiping her fingers wet with the speaker's juices on the speaker's thighs. Others form a part of her memory of self: a grandmother who holds proverbs that will carry meaning over time and generations, somehow warning her against sex with women and yet unable to change the desire ("A Ba A"), or an aunt who reminds her of the many ways in which seeing and not seeing are elemental to her sense of being a poet: "I want to tell him I am pained for looking. / I want to tell him to let his own eyes rest" ("Oji River Police College"). Finally, her aunt again gives explicit instructions, in one of the most affecting poems in the collection. In it we can see the wonderful way in which the poem enacts the wounding and healing that come with colonialism, sexism, migration, and the ordinary business of growing into one's art.

The aunt's wisdom is priceless, even when language stutters, struggles to find voice, the right word. She cautions, "I would not / curse my mother, as you too should know."

To curse one's mother is to curse one's making, and Danladi must struggle with this as a poet. At the end of it all is the sense that Danladi is deeply committed to exploring the meaning of a feminine voice—a woman's voice—in her work. "Let me weep," she says in "Oji River Police College," "to women's high worship, / rising from every church on every night."

SALT: ALUM

You can touch me.
I've been so good. I have
been especially
still, all this time,
each of my palms
made a bed for your untucking,

me, the meal made
from reused chicken grease:
eased and always saying yes.
Gender is cunning;
the ruination
unwitting—

a stolen position.
I have been bent over.
The beast dug
out of me, the jewels.

Pleasure light pops
the eyes, obsidian sticks in the throat,
even this body doesn't register.

The knuckles fold toward Lake Michigan.
The gut hardens.
Oxalate builds in the kidneys,
The tongue is a grateful peasant; for
a beating I can answer to a middle name.

ARPEGGIO

By now, everybody has gone home.
You and I remain with the messed
order of things. In the kitchen,
              bowl of fruit between us,
we try for a quarrel, one
row of murmurs following another, wondering
which overture tempers the excess.

Yours is the tongue lapping oil spilling from the rift.
What leaves my body is a remarkable
apparition, wholly resigned.
I reach out,
palm grief into an apple,
watch the space of your eyes coalesce
to tar pools.

We fools,
we've wounded the hunger in this room,
forgotten its commemoration.
I want nothing, in fact, but to pay
attention to the swelling.

We'll both seek sex after.
I'll turn my back to you,
you'll teeth the flesh of my neck,
offer my belly the embrace of a cold hand.

COMMUNION

I am not a woman afraid of her ghosts.
They feed me deep, settle deliberate
in the dermis, cloak me to health.
No one has a body that cannot be broken.
I shatter beneath a windowsill, separate as fruit
for provender: pomelo breasts,
lemondrop melon ass, a head
of ripened cantaloupe. My mouth
suckles a joint, sighs.
When I want the praise of generosity, I settle for men,
let barely boys meditate ocher flesh,
leak star milk into their laps,
permit them to call me mama, coat their mouths
citrus.
Who am I but a vessel for the pleasures of my haunts?
Meanwhile I imagine women
who have spread me sweet,
called me tangelo, burnt honey,
pomegranate marmalade,
gift me *sister* for company.
I am never abandoned, even
here, in my Champaign apartment:
topless-eating, falafel balanced on my chin,
poltergeists' moans as soundtrack,
synaptic pops bound endless for remembrance,
the body keeping vigil, my thighs a monastery,
ogogoro in the nook of my groin for libation.

PULL THE CORD

Mma has her fistula
oozing blue-black
cusped in palms, she says, *Come look.*

She ain't the type to
hold the blood too long, choosing
to drain veins pristine

most nights. Drinking coffee at
the kitchen table,
she does juju, skin falling

in clumps on cedar
tops. She curses, two fingers
out, *May you catch my*

pain, drink it all in, yambu.
Remember the gift I give.
I remember why I leave home.

Fingers coiled at my
neck, loosening the cord,
bloodied departure.

I'm allaying the armor.
Mma, have patience. Soon,
I promise to wear your wounds.

1998, I MISPLACED MY MOTHER IN UNION STATION

We've come to meet my father after work,
our guide who hides his accent behind prominent
incisors. Mma and me and sis are still heavy
with ours, heavy dark too from a stubborn

sun. Mma hands me one dollar for Oreos
which I've grown to love already. She says,
Sugar, love is what makes you American, sugar
and that hurried embarrassment of being seen

with her, so I rush around disrespectfully
like any American but Black-quiet.
I have my cookies and I shuffle on the tooth-
smooth steps past people who don't smell

like pepper or goat or the incense for Grandma's
health and I can't find Mma. I search all the Black
women's hands for clay-color henna, all their
feet for thirdhand K-Swiss, and I look up at the

ceiling's crinkled alabaster like the roof of a
mouth and start weeping and soon I'm on
First Street and I can't find my mma or
my sis either, matter of fact. A man in a

uniform accuses me, *What's wrong?* and
I've forgotten my good English already, then Mma
comes running at me and the man says to her,
You need to keep better watch of your

children, you foreigners can be so careless,
but Mma is already nodding so hard and cannot
efface any more before the cookies are crumbles
in my hands.

TOMORROW, CHAKA DEMUS WILL PLAY

while I braid my hair long / thump coconut oil between
the sections / crack palm nut with my teeth / rub the
meat on my belly / I'll want to go dancing / might
go to the Shake and Bake / I'll bless Ma with a salah /
tuck a miniskirt in my purse for later / might wear lip
-stick too / there'll still black henna on my hands from
Zaynab's wedding / they might bend around a black
man's waist / we'll dance like we're blood / we'll both
wonder / was the slave trader your ancestor or mine? /
his rum-laced tongue will coat my lobes / I'll think of
Mama / while he bonds with me / I can get home myself /
I'll say / I'll creep in / past Mama on the sofa / drink coffee
to mask the lust / oozing from me / I'll eat leftover jollof
cold from the pot / I'll heave / I might struggle / with sleep

PHENOMENOLOGY OF EXCESS

Everyone hasn't gone to the moon.
Some of us are still here,
Breathing heavy . . .

          —Essex Hemphill, "Heavy Breathing"

Light swallows cold the pooling sweat. Empty
canvases. I have three shades of lipstick.
All plum. Fog swirled me on the

way here. And I still smell like wet leaves.
Beyoncé, who I only tolerate,
careens overhead. Liquor has

been tender with me. This night in Chicago,
unrelenting queers do battle. I am
too dark for the studs. Too

femme for the femmes. Only the white
people want to take everything from me.
There must be something to fix.

I am the solemn carcass too sensitive
to be touched, reeking in the center of the room.
At the last call, a stranger puts three fingers in me

in the coat closet. She nuzzles me.
When she asks me my name I stutter.
She wipes my wetness on my thigh and laughs.

INHERITANCE

The reality that haunts is
the rocking chair, bathed in moon,
swaying by a window, on the second floor,
overlooking a field of white flowers.

This is not real.

In the dream,
the dog licks bathwater
from my calves,
falls ill the next day.

All to say I irritate the lining, then run loose.

My recent ultrasound reports three large
fibroids, a mouth holding jawbreakers
in the gums, raw red. A mouth
spurting blood clots.

Tell me something of history.

LEOPOLD II DEFENDS HIS PHILANTHROPY UNDER LE ASSOCIATION INTERNATIONAL AFRICAINE

Pleats. The folds are so important.
How skin settles in creases.
Flush with attention.
The way blades filet flesh from bone.
Holy aria in the bloom.

How can I explain this meat as a blessing?
A tracheal cutting. Minced sacrifice.
I am a giver of cauterized nubs.
Compatriots, feel free to call me hero.

And the rubber is nothing. Rite. Good feeling.
Wealth. I give the earth new limbs to knead
sacrifice. Collagenous tissue percolated in muck.
Weak carcasses a dark cutter.

A BA A

My grandmother was once a fura da nono seller in
Kaduna,
getting fat on cow butter. She gathered
bowls of the fermented milk, thought of her
descendants rotting in the New World.
For penance, she coated her gums with lime juice.
I pounded the pulp and rinds between my toes.

In my sleep a milk-drunk fly is incessant and wants to
tell me not to say *ira;*
the fly teaches me not to want but I am wanting;
the fly tells me, *She who eats will have no place name,*
that I might eat and be seared at the root.

a ba a—where one enters
ira—to lick; to have sex with a woman

19

OJI RIVER POLICE COLLEGE

In Enugu, the harmattan does not rage too harsh.
At 5:45 p.m., Aunty and I begin our walk, for 40 minutes,
a gleaming dusk eating our heels, our footsteps paced to match.
My skin rides on the teeth of biting flies, Aunty recalling
her day's due grievances and I am obliged to listen,
counting flecks of grayorange on lizards' backs.

She laughs at me often, saying,
Strange, my dear, these your eyes, they swallow everything.
My mouth, glum and outstretched, mutters an affirmation.
You must know that I began to lose my sight when I left this country.
Do you understand?

There is no quotidian.
Let me weep to women's high worship,
rising from every church on every night,
every sunset too winsome,
the burn of bitter leaf soup beguiling,
grant me use of sense I still maintain.

I find two cures for this.
The first: to wash my eyes of fog in the Oji River, and look fast to the sun.
The second: there is a small cluster of shops near the road
where men sell bread and okada fuel.
Aunty sends me to buy one loaf for tea,
a tin of malt chocolate.
I stop at a stand where the proprietor looks most like me.
He holds my hands before the naira, calls me sister.
When I am leaving, he calls me beautiful.

I want to tell him I am pained for looking.
I want to tell him to let his own eyes rest.

MY MOTHER'S SISTER SCHOOLS ME
ON HER GARDEN

Pay attention to the moringa saplings behind
those torn bricks; they were birthed on the eve
of bomb blasts, and are therefore always
anxious. See how they weep come any sound?

              Auntie wets her lips, continues.

To be this soil, here, at high noon the
day after a heavy rain, we could never
know the indulgence, the drunk delirium.
What is the word I am even looking for?

              It is something like rapture.

Do you know that we had been growing
potatoes since before the Irish came?
And they wailed from the sweetness of them.
Our earth is kinder, is why.

              A good earth reciprocates generously.

Also, it was these kasa beans that gave me teeth to
speak, to know the difference between
waace and uwaki, so that I would not
curse my mother, as you too should know.

E TU TU

After Chris Abani's "Benediction"

NEPA has taken light.
We fight mosquitoes in the dim fog that remains,
Auntie sucking the flesh of watermelon.
I watch her house girl break beans for soup.
I am playing with my tongue.
Each bean is   kpom kpom kpom   clicking against my teeth.
Auntie inches soft fruit toward me,
night heat gleaming in the swollen heat,
my noise against its backdrop begging
the sap of the sky for memory.
The training begins:
nga nga nganga becomes
a dance—of love and divination;
abu—is a song;
aba a o bia,
ichi icho echu—an initiation,
a search for, I will collect water;
aguu aguu aguru—there is a hunger if it remains.
          I am easily spun,   do I evoke
          a native dish or the best of my parts (oto otu)?
By the end it becomes:
evu avu ava—I am carrying a song of your name.

23

THE EARTH'S OWN ABOMINATION

Does it matter how you hung but that you
would have hung in any case?
When your body swung it swung a dance
of body love: your extended tongue kissing
your clavicle; the rigor of your erection
greeting the moon; your

noose and its embrace,
where we met.
You asked me to dance with you
for our sameness,
for dreaming the same demise: that
manipulated hope turned into an

endless hoover, imagine;
you, I know you
considered all that you may
sacrifice: your Ezinma alone,
Nwoye courting foreign flesh, before long
chanting the praise names of blanched gods,

the tragedy of choice.
I know you considered all you may gain:
meeting your mother again;
the ancestral realm;
Ikemefuna's embrace.
Forgive yourself

for forgetting what we inherit,

who we become.
Know that you are no more man
than your father, that
some lives are easier to end than live; in
certain hours, that is the truth of us.

Okonkwo, I know you loved that boy.
You will have your chance to speak with him again,
both of you dead by your hands,
some disquieted serenity.
Has his spirit yet paid you vigil?
The ants, the lizards? Other dead beneath you?

SAY MY NAME (1987)

i. Colonizer and I make our bed together.
I am at the point of begging now.

ii. My mother is a sand dune soaking in Manchester.
In the Northern Quarter she is letting white men taste her toes for practice.

iii. My father counts his lies in Lagos, or Washington last:
Here I no longer have to eat the bones of orphans;
I will water my garden with sea salt and grow yams to feed my children;
may the sun of this shore make limestone of my skin.
He tucks each one in the space between his teeth and sighs himself to sleep.

iv. Ibrahim Badamasi Babagida gets
his cock sucked as a reward for a bloodless coup and
Namesake has become Father of the House. Some say SAP means
Suffering for African People. But IBB still eats. More now.
Maryam says his cum tastes like roast lamb and coconut rice.

v. In Manchester, my mother considers gestation,
naming children in the cold.
After a pint of beer she thinks of proper titles: Miranda, or
Maggie Hilda. She moistens her lips with ice.

QUI PARLE

for Bouna Traore and Zyed Benna, whose deaths prompted the French riots of 2005

The boys offered their own benedictions, undeniably.
Who dreamed of becoming the martyr? The fear was

material and all they sought was home, a warm meal
from a warm woman to break the fast. Then,

midday came quick so even the ash caught fire.
Us? We hid in prayer and sleep. Do you know

the hollows the currents opened? All that remained
were the souls' etchings, the quintessence evaporated. All that

persisted was the heat. This being the foreign arrondissement,
even the passion ignited. Did you know the bodies swallowed

the power? Took all the light so the block may sit in darkness
with them. The transmission was simple, the moral:

the only way out of the banlieue is immolation.
Ma Bouna and Ma Zyed still had not taken the boys home.

The pure French refused to sell them magazines and food.
They bathed themselves Merlot red; we cloaked ourselves

in the night's ether. There was a plea to bury the bodies in moist
soil. La police in Clichy-sous-Bois licked blackblood from

their fingertips, smiled out loud, *Vive les français. Qui vit
est qui parle.* Les Africains murmured, *You cannot burn this hell*

further than it resembles. The bodies at rest are singed or weeping now.
A slow fire is eating at the hair and flesh. It bleaches the bones to white rubbish.

WHEN I FIRST ENCOUNTERED KWAME NKRUMAH'S CRYPT, I LAUGHED

The sun-blanched effigy gleamed,
the body of a haunt hot for wanting,
the crypt emerging that way
that wants to be seen in its unseeing,
if the unseen could ever be so humble.
They did not even let the man die here,
but there was love in the return, sure,
as I too have dug graves that hold no bones.
How many times must a man go on dying?
Could a father ever be that dead?
Would weeping be more appropriate?
Humor took hold as
I thumbed the fringe stones.
I left an offering of bronze.

Mine was the sun-blanched body,
skirting the pull of visibility
in a thrust the dead enact,
pretending to want to be forgotten,
as if we can shun character.
Osagyefo found his own end.
Consider the sweetness of forgiving.
Perhaps he is not even in there.
Perhaps he has gone on living elsewhere.
Is this the malediction of exile?
I should have wept more thoroughly but
I let the mirthful musing rack me.
The crypt is sanctuary for the displaced, I learn.
I hoped for a Kente inlay.

AT THE WORLD'S END

For (and after) Kofi Awoonor

At a soft shore,
I have the salt, a
boning knife, candles
(two red, one black), a spool of
thread. Easy waves wane, coax flitting
fish. I have the cry of the wind while the moon gives birth
in the offing. Boss, this now is my own lament. History reigns as
cruelty, consumes more than it kills. I croak with the kingfisher here, thirst sated,
hunger not, but seeking, this loss a continued meditation; the ache of the
   wound keeps me
up at night. Still I ask: What may I offer you? What would be enough? May I
   weep-sing
near Keta Lagoon? To hope that when the water breaks open there, people may
   hear the
heat of your name? Sir, even the ocean quavered, even death jostled. When my
wings mend, as night labors dawn, as the graves grow green, I will
burrow by the shoreline and meet you. I will have fruit and
sun and song for you. Here is peace, have it.

SUICIDAL IDEATION

I.

I must sing a bit for my own self. This
night, what I say in my meaningless
platitudes breeds exactly that: the feel of flat. This
night, I coat my teeth with my own intercessions:
I want to be big. I wish I was still a human.
I want to be a god in your cosmos. I want
to be   age old
milk wet   bone firm.
When I finish, imagine me hoary,
foul with my own being:
dirge   blood
salt   water
nothing of me crumbling for the
sea to shake loose. Let me become firm,
a stolid isle that breaks open the ocean.
I know that I could die here, consumed
and all-consuming.

II.

Crazed as we are, I do not fear for us, and it is as a
blessing. Come with me to fetch the dusk and tie its
seams to morning. Leave a trail of blood to keep warm
and remember the dreaming: I have skinned my frame
of flesh to remaining bones and found how black they
too were; with my palms and fingers frail, mind
bemused for the lack of sense, I opened my mouth to
my hands to collect my falling teeth. It was then that
I could speak freely. Dearest, come and lie with me:

me cold; you warm; in a cold bed; with warm blanket;
in a cold room still. I will let your deadening tongue lick
me peaceably until midday, toil the beat in our bellies
enough to pattern and make peace for our time left.

I USED TO BE CALLED OLIVIA

I dug my own unbecoming, as much as you:
thirst became ritual, the wallop of
water soaking into the earth, myself wafting off as dust—
an openness invited inward—blue, and enough.
I imagine childhood a swamp,
wet, my small self, nappy hair
doubled with cockleburs,
easy name lilting—spineless and clean—
muck sucking the shame quickly,
new abode forming, holding.

ACKNOWLEDGMENTS

"Tomorrow, Chaka Demus Will Play" first appeared in *PANK Magazine.*

GIRL B
VICTORIA ADUKWEI BULLEY

for Victor and Comfort and Mercy and Joseph
and the Others

This is a work of fiction. All names, characters, places, and incidents are a product of the author's imagination. Any resemblance to real events or persons, living or dead, is entirely coincidental.

Published by Akashic Books
©2017 Victoria Adukwei Bulley

ISBN: 978-1-61775-567-5

Akashic Books
Brooklyn, New York
Twitter: @AkashicBooks
Facebook: AkashicBooks
E-mail: info@akashicbooks.com
Website: www.akashicbooks.com

African Poetry Book Fund
Prairie Schooner
University of Nebraska
110 Andrews Hall
Lincoln, Nebraska 68588

TABLE OF CONTENTS

What does it mean to grow up in contemporary Britain as a young woman of African heritage? What happens when the body responds to notions of beauty and self-worth imposed by a systemically racist Western paradigm? Is compromise necessary if we are to survive this world of technologized modernity? How do we love—our parents, friends, partners, God (whether Buddhist, Islamic, Christian, or Pagan)? And how might poetry begin to redress these sociocultural, political, spiritual, and gender-skewed imbalances? These are some of the questions that preoccupy the British-Ghanaian poet Victoria Adukwei Bulley in *Girl B*—a probing, thoughtful, and quietly exhilarating debut. I use the word *quietly* with a little reservation, as these are not slight poems: Bulley's ambition and reach is impressive and she makes her point in a manner that is enviably subtle yet direct.

In the opening "Girl"—which reads as both self-portrait and a retrospective letter to a younger self (while simultaneously recalling a more generic everywoman of color)—Bulley contemplates the physical in language that makes you sit up and pay attention. This is a place where "the grasp of your jeans" is "at you like a lover you'd like to leave," where (moderately) aging limbs are "fighting baby jihads against lipids." Similarly, in the following "Luna" she renders fresh familiar territories such as the discourse surrounding the female body, menstruation, fertility, and their relationship to the moon. Here, a larger concept of matriarchal embodiment is expertly counterpointed against a "brutal and unforgiving" science capable of capturing ovulation on camera, yet failing to answer any of the questions real women and girls might put to it. The black woman's body as political battleground is explored further in the four-part "Girls in Arpeggio," which takes the reader from the "Early Intervention" of children's hair relaxers, where :

The smiles of the girls

5

on the children's relaxer kits
told no lies. They were too happy
to realise they were poster girls
for the effacement of themselves.

to the closing "Realpolitik," in which a nonracialized, self-governed reappropriation of beauty becomes a "violent" yet satisfying act. The notion of effacement/disappearance is pushed even further in "Girl Gone," where the discovery of a woman's body prompts the poet to first pray "don't let it be her" and then to conclude that if the body was not "hers," whomever that might be, then "still somebody else / waits in water for the sound of a name / mispronounced on registers, / missing from news."

Elsewhere, nature as a biological entity is an important and active agent in the drama, and it is explicity explored as a construct in "Lost Belonging," which utilizes the concrete to mirror London's tallest skyscraper, the Shard, and the angular aggressions that the structure has come to symbolize. Whether it is politics or metaphysics, Bulley is unafraid to stare down the big issues and take them to task: alongside beauty, she also considers mortality and love. "This whole impermanence thing is deceptive," she writes in "Fifteen," a gentle elegy to a childhood friend/admirer. One of the most affecting and personally nuanced poems in the book is "Peach Crayon," where she expresses doubt about being in a (loving) mixed black/white relationship because their offspring will inevitably have to face "Everything // but us, from Disney to Hitler," telling them to "process the brown // out of themselves / like bread, like rice."

In this sense, Bulley's thematic concerns are not dissimilar to British diasporic writers such Malika Booker or Warsan Shire, both of whom are fellows of the UK development program The Complete Works. However, in terms of style and approach, Bulley is quite distinct. As she is a new participant in the scheme, it will be interesting to see how her voice and enthusiasms develop after a year's intensive mentoring. I suspect that her innate capacity for narrative and laser-sharp eye for detail, coupled with a speculative and naturally inquiring disposition, will blossom further as she engages with the formal opportunities that poetry uniquely offers.

The penultimate poem, "Blue, Like Cerulean," is one of the more elusive pieces in the book, yet ironically it is probably closest to an *ars poetica* in a metaphorical sense. The "you" as apostrophe might be read as the poet as individual, womankind in a universal sense, or as the titular "Girl B" as emblematic African woman. While the addressee is identified as "the baby of returnees" and "the bloodlet future / of the Malê Revolt"—a slave uprising in Bahia, Brazil—which led to the deportation of its leaders to the West African coast—it is language, the tool and weaponry of the writer, that offers a form of resolution. As a continuum that accompanies the diasporic traveller on her or his eternal journey "home," it is ever-present, and can be found, on demand, as "a key in the porch / just under the rug."

GIRL

Hair coming down past your breasts like confetti. Your straighter teeth, your stripped upper lip (recoiling still), your clean, dark complexion. Lean thighs, or the gap between them. The grasp of your jeans at you like a lover that you'd like to leave, exposing the gap. The sign between your feet pointing upward, *tear here.* Sun, sea, sand, shea butter, you are smoother skin, sanded nails, dark eyes seeing almonds. Your voice, your vocal chords, stroked by secondhand smoke. Your dozy tongue, stacking it over words you really should know how to pronounce by now. And feet, lithe, slim, no peeling, arches secure as scaffolds. Oiled joints, humming the silence of youth. Limbs fighting baby jihads against lipids, still winning. Your heart still kicking it in time, red metronome, your shunning of the night; a propensity for wakefulness, for pen against paper—a dance of sorts—because what is death to you?

(break)

My sweet girl.

(break)

Will you write to me, years from today, when you no longer are what you are now? I'd like to know what you'll be.

(break)

Call me when you find out.

(break)

I'll be here.

LUNA

By sleeping in the dark, said Louise,
a girl realigns her chemicals according
to the clock face of old. With a pair of heavy curtains

and a thermometer, she maps her inbuilt
almanac to a graph and then divines, from this,
the times when she is most magical. This dreamtime

troubles the veil between worlds, incites visions,
can slam oceans against coastlines
like jealous lovers. Man, let a girl feel this amber sphere

just once, and she'll forget what she heard about God
and her body; seeing what difference is left, knowing
how books have burned over both. Science, too:

brutal and unforgiving—until it got the eclipse on camera:
the follicle exploding like bubble wrap,
the ballooned egg in release,

until the window for conception slams shut
faster than Pandora's trinket box, or the door of an aircraft,
One small step for man, one giant leap,

but when us girls were at school, we spoke of our own landings
plainly. If at all, as weeds, as inconvenient blossomings,
marooning the flowerbed, claiming what wanted

only to be good, clean fun, leaving
a crimson imprint after slipping in, noiseless, uncalled for,
unnamed, through the night, like a new moon.

LOST BELONGING

I
left
my bag
on the train
under the table.
Forgot it, looking
at the sun as I rolled
home into the city. Gold
was spilling from the frame
of a skyscraper and it looked
like a fire but it was only nature
reflecting off of steel. It was nature,
at it again, refracting from the metals
of this skin that we have grown so lately.
Everything is going to break and I must get
home before it does, or doesn't yet, or buckles.
Back to the snug shut door, to the batteries +/−
all dashed from the clock and the blinds closed tight,
a millipede of stinging eyes, red light crashing through
from the realm behind them. *Mother. Where else can I go?*

FIFTEEN

With a hopscotch grid for a wrist,
see my sad boy

with a smile like a one-string guitar
relative to nobody, yet out of tune,

dropping out of school
out of line, saying,

I love you more than life itself,
in a first Valentine's card

during the spring term
in which we turn fifteen.

In the attic of an old phone, now,
here he is again

in the drawer I was cleaning out
during a hymn I was singing

before I met him,
and here he is, my sad boy—

now watch this older girl stop
and cast her day out with the dust

and become sad too.

This whole impermanence thing is deceptive.
Looks lifelong, actually, to me,

sat here still molding mason jars
of words to preserve him with,

wondering if a poem ten years on
is still a pining, asking

how many more I will make
before I learn how little of us keeps.

LIMINAL

Some things
you learned early
and quietly.

Via
no vote, referendum
or consensus,
skirts rolled up at the waists,
beltlines curled over themselves
like puckered lips,
hemlines lifting like smoke—
no fire,

       Girl, where did you get that smile from?

Skirt hems
border between two countries
that aren't friends—
just a little fun,
modesty in remission: last row
of the crop before the prairie ends,
then, moving up, up, in the world
like a safety curtain,

       But when are you sixteen though?

Nothing wrong to be done here,
much worse than bad grades,
and you're top of the class,
so,

You don't say much, do you?

Smart, but too shy.
Lips all shut. Mouth peanut
tied tight like a top button.
Tongue tired like
shoelaces dragged through
dirt, but,

Don't you want to?

Notice
this thick, red theater curtain rise—
behind it:
all Oz,
no wizard, no witch,
no lie,
no Tigger,
no teddy bears here, no,

just something you don't know
how to use yet, don't know
the depth of, don't know
how to love, just know
how to sell.

GIRL GONE

Morning
and they say
they've found a body
and I begin to pray, inwardly moan,
God, don't let it be her,
let this not be a rebirth
of grief.

Most mornings,
not too tired, I complete my entreaty
to the great silence, but today
the note goes unstamped a few words short
of an *amen*.

See this, now,
my latest sinning: accepting the alchemy
of souls into strata, as though regimental,
unquestioning. I was almost a good girl,
a good subject,

thinking it makes no difference
whose life-loss they speak of
on the radio—whose negative space wins
the chalk lining of talk.

As far as love knows, it *is* all the same.
If not her, someone else.
If not hers, still somebody else
waits in water for the sound of a name
mispronounced on registers,
missing from news.

WHAT IT MEANS

The campus nurse offers up pills
like penny sweets.

Means it when she says
it's just one less thing to worry about.

It's okay.
There are many freedoms.

In the first world,
freedom from bloodshed

is tasted
between the legs.

I don't judge.
How would she know

I have come to love
the cup spilling over:

the floor of the bath
a Rothko on fiberglass,

an opening ceremony,
a private showing

circa this month.
There is little like knowing

17

I am an orchestra—
only rehearsing.

GIRLS IN ARPEGGIO

1. Early Intervention

The smiles of the girls
on the children's relaxer kits
told no lies. They were too happy
to realize they were poster girls
for the effacement of themselves.

Not knowing this either,
we would sit there, still,
watching our mothers mix dreams
with a spatula; watching the mirror
from under the eaves
of our alkaline cream caps.
We stared at the girl on the box, willing
to be cleaned before sin,
and as the soft, pink science got working,
pleasantly tickling the skin, we waited
until our blood-borne bonds would break
just enough, perhaps,
for all in the world that resisted us
to straighten out.

2. Forbearance

There is a toll charged
for choosing to be the exotic one.
The problem has something to do

with your acceptance of a cage
made from laundered gold.

birds of paradise,
you were the first dreams to die
when the ships arrived / and when
they arrived / they belonged / and you
did not belong / unless
you belonged
to
them.

3. Forgiveness

Oh daughters of Eve,
did you know
you were a quarter-formed thing?
Or did you never pull the wings
off a fly, one by one, and wonder
what to name it then?

Or did they only tell you and tell you
walk tall; hold your heads high,
you sweeter berries, you
picked-too-soon,
and placed in the heat to dry
and stain the pavement
apologetically.

4. Realpolitik

Somewhere beyond the last of the pencil lines   tattooed
onto the doorframes of their kitchens   their only nations, these girls,   cacao-cored
and peppercorn pin-curled, decided to call themselves   beautiful.
Not   chocolate or caramel. Not coconut or tan. Not Bounty, not Hovis best-of-both
or burnt wholemeal toast. Not Oreo or Coco Pops. Not buff nor carbon-cum-diamond
blick. Not lighty   not pick 'n' mix and match   not hair enough to hang from.
Not video girl. Not side chick. Not thick. Not booty or apple-bottom. Not deputation
any longer, not another   word   not vice, not hereafter any cover-teacher
or stand-in nor prefix; no sign nor understudy, no other   for *beauty*
anymore.

For these girls it was a violent act.
But after it, they slept better.

RETREAT

4.

Ruby says nothing.

Ruby cuts a tube of penne in half with the side of her fork, a slow-motion blade stooping to kiss the back of my neck. A warning. *Eat, before it gets cold; before you forget how to do it.* Until now, I jigsawed her exposition to find the best fit. Satisfied, I clean my plate.

3.

I haven't seen a wasp in years, but there are *wasps* here, larger than the ones I remember. Padma, our retreat leader, climbs the bunk bed, removes a hornet from the room with a cup.

2.

Evan is a sixty-five-year-old retired father, just like Dad. *You remind me of my dad,* I tell him, *the only difference being, of course, that you're white.*

4.

Everybody has bought and is studying one of the many dharma books on sale here, except Alastair, 84, who reads Alastair Cook instead.

5.

I am in the shrine room, closest to Buddha, when Evan is crying. We two are the last ones left, but the room—though vacant—is loud with her, humming, *Sarah, Sarah,* between each caught breath.

1.

The week begins when I turn off my phone. I delete the world as an infant does. I keep my palms flush over my eyes, until I realize I do not own a watch or an alarm clock.

8.

Brother, may you be well. May you be happy. May you be free from suffering.

7.

On the last evening, a sunset. My turn in the kitchen. Ruby offers to take my shift, so that I can walk with the others. It is the first time she's volunteered to speak to me, and when she calls me, I hear it like a song, and begin to love my name.

6.

Barbora waves until my rearview mirror swings her face and wind-up hand out of sight. I will see her again, several times. I don't know this. Or, too, that she will even visit my house, sit with me on the floor of my parents' room, where it is quiet. Or that whenever I picture her, no matter how much in the future, she will always be waving goodbye.

DIPTYCH

MYTHOLOGY

Mythology is the bread of this nation. They make new ones, every morning, which they forget by tomorrow. This present state of recall is archipelagic. But myths demand memory, need kneading to survive. The last time I flew, Grandpa asked Uncle, my Dad, my cousins, and I if we were his children. Our *yes* was a yeast-like yes. We were myths in flesh, raising his spirit to say, *Well, in that case, we thank God.*

TRADITION

Tradition is a step in time that ends decades of roaming for a place unnamed on a modern map. The songs they used to sing there, with a rhythm you still dance to. Watch *kpanlogo* and see. Mind the beat. The feet have muscle memory. They testify to the dust. Tread bloodlines between the past and present and, maybe, from the wrong side, maybe they will not touch freedom. But *ka akaa akwëö*, nonetheless.

PEACH CRAYON

All your love aside,
I thought about leaving you

for some imaginary man:
tall, dark, hair like mine

but cut back, shaped up, black, too.
I was thinking about the kids—

about the kids of the kids.
It seemed the safest way

to ensure they won't come home
like I did, bearing artwork, portraits

of the artists: white and blond,
aquamarine gems for eyes

in place of obsidian, too young
to call it surrealism. Everything

but us, from Disney to Hitler,
will tell them to process the brown

out of themselves
like bread, like rice. From birth,

everywhere will say,
Little brown thing

cut your husk off,
trim your crusts off,

them bits there are only
for feeding to the birds.

POLAROID

You and him and two or three kids. Two girls and a boy. The twins, and then the boy, so no one ever felt alone or replaced. You are standing by the lake. It is sunny and you are all brown and you are all browner than yesterday, and grinning.

Maybe this vacation is in Africa. Maybe it is where you live. None of you stand out from the other through blurred eyes. You each have a fist raised up, and it is not a Kodak statement, nor is it saying cheese. It is the exclamation mark at the end of your statement, which is that you are brown, and so is he, and this is Africa, and these are your kids. And that is all. Or everything.

BLUE, LIKE CERULEAN

Did they know the land you grew up in?
Did they watch from above the water,
you moving about their waists

like distorted fish—baby gold koi coasting
black-hole-mouthed at the surface,
bigger when viewed askew?

Seems they came in from the red sand,
birthed you in the water, and you grew gills, girl,
time ago, but in your sleep

you still say don't leave me here.
You turned four, learned to add
dates of birth and wait on loneliness,

but your people are not nomadic—
why must you be homeless now?
In your blood you are a pagan

a Mohammedan, a Hebrew,
a lover of Christ—
why would you choose now?

You are the baby of returnees:
you are the bloodlet future
of the Malê Revolt, always

forever going home
with language, a key in the porch
just under the rug.

TERMINAL INDEX

So far, what I have
is you, Dad, migrating
from sitting room, bottom right-hand
side of the house, two floors skyward
to the loft, then back earthbound
to catch signal,

       Hello!
    Onouhi, onouhi?
           Can you hear me?

And though my sides split and
leak laughs onto the Internet
at this telecom farce, I will know
what that phrase means
for what's left of my life.

And then you, Mum, downstairs
with a more local transmission,
phone warm at your cheeks'
clan marks, now transmitters
breathing,

     Ohh wohyémi,
       I am well.
           God is good.

Or you, Mum, with me
on the floor of the kitchen,

my kneecap a bar of soap ablaze,
my mouth a chimney of howl,
and your

     Kpo . . . kpo . . .

conjured to end pain,
unspill milk, or unspool thread
tied too tautly around a bale
of braided hair.

So far, my menagerie of terms is
small fragment, speck, found object,
sound, word, and phonic,
but I keep it.

Collect, collect, collate
and conceal it—under head and pillow
just as Grandma caches money
in case she ever needs it.
In case it one day grows.

NOTES

Ka akaa akwëö: a Ga proverb, meaning, *Let us at least try and see.*

Malê Revolt: From the Yoruba term *imalé*, for *Muslim*. An 1835 slave revolt in Bahia that led, in part, to the deportation of its surviving leaders to the West African coast.

BONE LIGHT
YASMIN BELKHYR

Published by Akashic Books
©2017 Yasmin Belkhyr

ISBN: 978-1-61775-564-4

Akashic Books
Brooklyn, New York
Twitter: @AkashicBooks
Facebook: AkashicBooks
E-mail: info@akashicbooks.com
Website: www.akashicbooks.com

African Poetry Book Fund
Prairie Schooner
University of Nebraska
110 Andrews Hall
Lincoln, Nebraska 68588

TABLE OF CONTENTS

PREFACE
by Ladan Osman

Yasmin Belkhyr has titled her chapbook as if naming one of the girls flitting through her speaker's dreams. *Bone Light* is porous and amorphous, exploring lines between the material and immaterial. These poems seem polite, straightforward. Then we find sticking blood, scabs, rust, and teeth everywhere. We finish and ask: what happened, who caused these marks, what wore away these figures, this speaker? When said aloud, the title encourages a boundary between words. In that equation, *Light* is the suggested denominator hovering underneath. There are physical and psychic bounds affecting the girls and women described here. But the speaker, with all her births, her multiplications into babies and girls, figures it all. Mark-making and tallying injuries, moments of respite.

The chapbook opens with an interesting disparity. The aggrandizement of titling this poem after the first chapter of the Quran, and the presentation of a speaker who is nameless, who is unable to list, who can't see her reflection, who may stumble in prayer, who is sick, afraid, who remembers clearly what she *never* saw, who wouldn't know, who didn't even know. This accumulation of uncertainty, this undermining of voice, is common in contemporary poetry, but Belkhyr pursues undercuts to a nearly absurd degree, toward surrealism. Belkhyr has made subtle and technically bright choices: the speaker doesn't know in the conditional / the speaker didn't know in the past but can now measure her not-knowing. "Not even," implies these obscurities challenge her stability. This work with ideas of knowledge and the reliability of this container of knowledge is, finally, humble. We ask along with her: How *do* you hold something like that? How does this world hold us?

The speaker may be unable to answer this question, but in her wisdom she seems unwilling to try. We observe girls and women in the social and political landscapes of Morocco and the United States. We observe them in the intimate space of the poem, noting their physical proximity to lame horses, dogs, and slaughtered farm animals. In "Laylat Al-Qadr," the speaker says: "If I throw a nickel off the bridge, I'm thinking about my niece." The greater environment, the speaker, and the graphic space of the poem acknowledge tight bounds, female closeness to bad omens. This poem is named after a chapter in the Quran as well as an Islamic high holy night. It's usually translated as "The Night of Power." In Belkhyr's work, the "unnatural," rather than the supernatural, causes what festers to "dampen and quiet." The city, wounded dogs, and children are strangely inert. If scripture delivers exacting decrees in Arabic, this speaker remains undefined in form and voice. She reads to a girl in English, a foreign tongue. It's partition on partition, a nearly suffocating quieting. In the poem before this, "Eid Al-Adha," named after a Muslim festival marked by charity and communal meals, there's no sense of celebration. Only resignation. The speaker recites: "I mean, burn the car and all its histories. I mean, nosedive into the lake and come out when it's good and quiet. Ugly duckling and all that." She puts out the fire of her own image. She renders herself nearly totally in the physical, and further, insults that form.

Belkhyr follows these poems with meditations on fathers and daughters. This may be read as a larger mediation on women and the law, family structure as parable to get at the philosophies that inform gender imbalance. The festival Belkhyr mentions earlier also recognizes Ibrahim's (Abraham's) will to sacrifice his son. "Interlude with Forgotten Myth, or, Portrait of Ibrahim's Daughter" offers no mercy:

> I have a recurring dream in which my father breaks the
> neck of every pigeon in the park. I help: a good daughter. I
> snatch them from the air & tear out the feathers. Bloody.
> In the stories, there was a king named Ibrahim & he
> loved his god.

"In the stories" girls like her kill alongside their fathers, handle guns, frequent dirty places, sweat. They're not worthy of the altar of sacrifice, or if they are, the sacrifice is living, ambiguous. Their actual deaths are not worth mentioning. This is true for girls and women of color, from occupied states across the Middle East to marginalized American communities. There's a persistent inanity around definitions, value: A monster's aide. Or an insignificant monster. "No one calls me foreign but I know that's what they mean." Then, "all" and "always" don't signal confidence, knowing. Their use signals negation of a wider story. Of course, a speaker who doesn't believe in her limitlessness, in space for her story's singularity, doesn't recognize the All, doesn't make God a proper noun. This speaker becomes subject to the restrictions of political and emotional realms. "My father was dead or the king or a god." ("& the Song of the Swan Drifts") A man may be a god but the women are women, are linked to girls, and do not or cannot behave much differently. A turn to a limiting story and self-description is a trauma more total than any imaginable. This "violence is universal." It takes up her whole universe.

Now this body, contained by form and by story, enters an uncomfortable reality. In "& the Riad Stole Our Breath," Americans are white (otherwise, why is the brownness of the boys remarkable?). This erasure is so shocking and reads as so automatic, it may as well be *an event*. A Big Bang that scours the melting pot so it shines white. The Americans are in physical and emotional contrast to our speaker: they are sensible, "clean." Even their language is clean. We can imagine them as an Adam and Eve, beings on the edge of chaos, standing court in a riad. "I pray, violently, that they get worms." This subversive gesture doesn't correct for the subjugation depicted here. The strangeness is that the boys are also First Human figures, pineapple soda their apple. So who is the speaker? "Even here, she is a stranger. The hard cost of English, tongue betraying the skin" ("Our Mothers Fed Us Well"). Streets wind through cities, vehicles hurtle through and around them, stray dogs walk and sleep. The speaker roams notions of home in similar ways. She's a stranger everywhere. There are so many kinds of exile. There are so many ways to lose refuge.

"This is how we live: chasing or chased" ("Jamilah Sweeps the Rubble"). The night quiets, takes "empty" and "closed" mouths. Night, and perhaps bodies, are black (or at least dark) and closed; on a number line, as in compound inequalities, the value is included at the interval. Belkhyr keeps her instrument, her specificity, her value intact:

I don't scream, pull the throat out of my voice.

This collection further acquaints us with an emerging poet, editor, and thinker. Yasmin Belkhyr is "green-mouthed," spending hours "watching the trees undress." She has the right recitations and the right voice for her landscapes. There's litter and commotion agitating her speaker's internal and external lives, but Belkhyr maintains her composure through acts of questioning, witness, and delineation.

ONE

SURAH AL-FATIHA

In my earliest memory, a man slaughters a goat in my bathroom. In Rabat, I am nameless, another Moroccan girl to be looked at but not seen. When goats cry, it sounds just like a baby. I couldn't list all the terrible things we do to one another. I remember the goat kicking out, frantic. The shattered mirror. The stumbled prayer. I was sick every visit: my stomach heaving dirty water. I would cry and everyone else would *tsk*, murmur *American*. Once, I kissed someone and I'm afraid it ruined the world. I've learned that it's not what you do with the knife—it's how you hold it after. But how do you hold something like that? Something that never stops baring its teeth; a voiceless dog, all bite, no bark. I remember very clearly that I never saw any blood. Honestly, I wouldn't even know what to do with a knife. I didn't even know what to do with that mouth.

BONE LIGHT

There are moments when I don't know if I'm sleeping or not. Moments where I wake up with another version of myself lying on top of me, her head resting on my belly. Sleep-doused girls with my big nose and big eyes and curly hair. Every year, my mother celebrates the anniversary of her miscarriages. Shoe boxes of ultrasounds, fruit tart from the diner with the scabbed leather booths. We don't throw out much around here. Wipe the plates clean. When the girls finally sleep, I put my fingers in their mouths and check for rotten teeth. People spent centuries debating the difference between a gift and a lame horse. Most nights, I watch movies where strangers fall in love then destroy each other. No one wanted that dog to die. No one ever wants the dog to die.

FISHTAIL BY THE SYCAMORE

There are so many things I want. Sometimes I worry my face betrays it all, that huddled strangers on the subway can see me for what I am. Green-mouthed and frothing. Quietly imploding. There are a lot of things my mother doesn't know about me. I put my phone number on Internet forums. I use tampons and smoke menthols. I can't remember the name of my biological brother. What kind of person does that make me? Occasionally, men call me late at night and tell me about their days. I only hang up when they ask me for my name or tell me theirs. Once, there was a horse and it walked into the ocean and I didn't say a word. I spend hours watching the trees undress. That's all autumn is really. What's in your mouth or the idea of a mouth.

TWO TRUTHS & A MOUTH OF LIES

I don't stay up late anymore. I've always liked my hands. There's nothing I'd enjoy more than a man who wants me. When they took it out of me, I thought I'd feel worse. It worries me how calm I am in the face of imminent disaster. These are the questions that lull me to bed: Will we recognize each other in heaven? How much does one need to lose to lose themself? Why don't I tip more? I am churning with want, but not the kind you think. My mother cries over me more often than I admit. A boy kissed a boy against the fence behind the pool. I can't explain death to anyone, least of all myself. I smile at strangers. When I was told the truth, I broke the mirrors and sobbed. I saw a man on a bike get hit by a car today. I don't mean a thing I say.

EID AL-ADHA
After Luther Hughes

There are so many bodies of mine that I haven't claimed yet. So many versions, so many lives. Fat purple figs and all that. When I speak of bodies, I mean: I'm afraid of mine. When I speak of bodies, I mean: I wonder what yours is capable of. When I speak of bodies, I mean: there is too much inside of me. I mean, burn the car and all its histories. I mean, nosedive into the lake and come out when it's good and quiet. Ugly duckling and all that. When I speak of bodies, I mean: I've never seen one that isn't alive. I mean, when the boy died, the coffin was closed. Everything we do to one another can be explained by love. Even violence. Especially violence. Nothing could be more satisfying than that. In a fever dream, we were on a road in Bouznika and the water seemed endless.

LAYLAT AL-QADR

I don't own any mirrors. In sleep, I scrape ticks off the windows. Once, a bird startled itself into the apartment and I was alone. If I throw a nickel off the bridge, I'm thinking about my niece. While the city slept, sound dripped slow down the street. An unnatural thing. The festering mess to suddenly dampen and quiet. None of the wounded dogs moaned. None of the children woke curled around ghosts. During the day, I wore a loose dress and bought pastries from a bakery and thought of all the people I'd like to touch. At night, I imagined the ways I could sink. My little fears and aches, the stupid rust in my chest. Define: daughter. Define: obligation. Define: heartless. I swear, I'd be better if I could. The girl was named Rumisa and I read to her in English and that's all you need to know.

INTERLUDE WITH FORGOTTEN MYTH, OR, PORTRAIT OF IBRAHIM'S DAUGHTER

I have a recurring dream in which my father breaks the neck of every pigeon in the park. I help: a good daughter. I snatch them from the air & tear out the feathers. Bloody. In the stories, there was a king named Ibrahim & he loved his god. No one calls me foreign but I know that's what they mean. In the stories, girls like me sweat out the fevers, drop dirty guns in the trash chute. We rip the rabbit's heart right out of its fucking chest. All that red-soaked skin under our fingernails. All I do is think about stories. About history, or his story, or her story, or my story. They're all the same story really. Someone always ends up holding something mangled.

TWO

& THE SONG OF THE SWAN DRIFTS

When I was alone in the city, every man spoke my name. Called me rivergirl, mouthsore. Habiba. Habibti. The ovens flared and spit, slabs of meat browning, boys with seaborn eyes slapping the air with folded newspapers. Bees dozed around the hot mess of honey and butter, and I have a woman's body but a girl's voice when I ask for chebekia, for zmita, for m'smmen. Beyond us, the goats wailed. Tails swinging at mosquitoes swollen lazy with their blood. Portraits of our king in every doorway. Every man I walk by imagines our children, his hand on my waist. My mother was in Taza or Casa or New York. My father was dead or the king or a god. A bushel of mint cost me one dirham. The family next door caught me smoking out the window. Later that night, I thought I was dying. I remember lying on the bed, clenching my stomach and thinking, *I am dying*. Every night that week, I had the same dream: a man knee-deep in water, his hand in my mouth, pushing my teeth into my teeth.

& MY FATHERS RELIVED MY BIRTH

12 years old and I was as bad as my aunts said. In Taza, we went to my uncle's wedding. We slept in a small hotel and I poured warm milk off the balcony. I stole all the chocolates from the front desk. I was kind to the bride but I cursed in English. I spit zuriya'ah seeds everywhere. I ate more than my share. *Aa'weeli, hashooma, Yasmin, baraka aleek.* This part is blurry: thick slaps of blood on the staircase. They slaughtered the cow on the roof before the wedding. Later that night, my uncles danced. In dreams, the cow comes back to life over and over, her eyes as dark as my own.

& THE BRIDE OF THE NORTH MOURNS

In Tangier, brownfleck geese dip their wings in the fountains. The children here beg. In my mouth, a peach bursts from its skin. A scar cuts the cheek of a ten-year-old. The sea is young and green. There is a blind woman singing. Darija skips across the air. His bride was pretty, wide-hipped; her father was known. His bride was 15. The children have black teeth. The sunsets go on for years. The riad was built with blood money. The riad has tulips, velvet and sweet.

& THE RIAD STOLE OUR BREATH

In another memory, Americans offer a bottle of pineapple soda to two brown boys in a town outside Marrakech. They scuffle, the glass shattering against the ground. Twining trees lope over garden fences, peaches just out of reach. Behind them, the Americans gasp sensibly, clean hands over clean mouths. The fist of a child is a terrible thing. The blood of a child is a terrible thing. Sweet and sticky pineapple clogs the air. The Americans murmur in their clean language and walk away. I am 14 years old and as petty as they come: that night, I pray, violently, that they get worms.

& WE HAVE NEVER OWNED CASABLANCA

It's hard to find work, a man on the train tells me. He asks if I am married, if I have a boyfriend. *I'm seeing someone*, I lie. We are cramped together in the doorway, late August, the train a bullet streaking to the airport. My suitcases are between us, his mother sitting beside the door. Miles sweep by, sea becoming country becoming city becoming sea again. Here, it all leads to water. *They're building a new city. Between Kenitra and Mehdia*, he says. *Piece by piece, the cities reach for each other.* The train jolts: he grabs my arm, steadies me, horribly intimate. *I could build*, he says, *but my hands are too soft.* Outside the window, a flash of children chase chickens in a grassless yard. *Do you like strong men?* He has a stain on his shirt and moist palms. His mother smiles at me, squeezes her son's arm. She offers me a warm date, a firm strawberry. *I think you are very beautiful*, he says. *What is your name?* The train slows to a stop: outside, the waves thrash against the rocks, beating them smooth.

& THE SONG OF THE CROW SHRIEKS

The dead girl didn't die. Her only burden was a stubborn tongue, her mouth a cluster of broken moons. The dead girl picked apples, cut her fingers, let the blood drip into the pie. Golden and brown, gorgeous in summer light. In myth, she was a stream of honey. In myth, her palms held ruins. In myth, they called the dead girl River and she bled and bled and bled.

THREE

MENARA GARDENS

If you dissect the poem, this is what you will find: a handful of broken glass, bottles of rosewater, an olive branch. I bought Rumisa yogurt. I bought Adnane ice cream. Messy baby mouths. I called her sister. I forgot to call. I didn't forget to call. I just didn't call. If you crack an egg, something spills. I try for honesty. I slept on the couch because they had no bed. If you dissect the poem, this is what you will find: the moon crumbling into the sea. All of my names spread like a deck of cards. Watch as I make you disappear. It is hard to love a history you do not know. If you dissect the poem, this is what I will hide: the phone call in which I asked my grandfather to pick me up early. When we watched American comedies, they always laughed a moment too late. Thin slices of lemon next to the kofta. The moon outside, a white vein, the strongest rib.

CANDID OF MERYAM, WITHOUT ANY REMORSE

My aunt speaks to me in English before she leaves, has me promise I won't leave the apartment once night comes. When she is gone, Meryam offers to take me out. Dusk arrives, and we walk to the Medina. She has wrapped a hijab around her henna'd hair. Adenane is running into the street on his baby legs, hurling pebbles at a stray dog. A man is leaning against a wall, staring at Meryam, a strange look on his face. Rumisa is singing to herself, a nonsense song in English I taught her hours before. *Reeng roud rosy, reeng roud rosy.* The man's eyes flicker from Meryam to Rumisa. *Shcoun hedek rajuul?* I ask. *Who is that man?* She glances briefly, tightens her grip on her daughter's hand. *No one*, she tells me in Arabic. *I loved him*, she says. Beyond us, I see the dog limping away—no wounds, just ache.

SIDI ALI

My brother brought me kofta and fresh mangoes. He slept in the smallest apartment I've ever seen—a room, really, underneath the butcher's shop. I have forgotten his name. I brought him pants last summer. They fit him well. He smelled like fresh meat. He was sleeping when I first came to Salé, wouldn't wake up, not even for me. He calls our mother *Jamilah*, same as Meryam, same as me. He brought me a bracelet from the beggars by the mosque. He refused my money. We watched action movies together because through our many languages, violence is universal. When we broke our fast, I always ate first. We had nothing to say to each other. In the end, we had nothing to say to each other.

JAMILAH SWEEPS THE RUBBLE

In dreams, my father has his back to me. When I asked Jamilah for his name, she said nothing. Lost in translation. In dreams, the dog finally bites, teeth caught on soft skin. I don't scream, pull the throat out of my voice. My father walks through the Medina, twisting into the snake of this city. I follow, every road winding, the stone walls high and narrow, washed white and pale blue. This is how we live: chasing or chased. I hear barking, smell blood. In dreams, my cousin shoots the dog, and I tend to my wounds. When I finally reach my father, he is at the edge of the cliff. *Turn around*, I say. *What is my name?* I say. The sky is dark as a closed fist. The ocean becomes a palm. Every dream holds petals of truth. Before my father falls, he turns. He has no face: only a mouth, closed.

SALÉ, 2013

I can justify every terrible thing I've ever done. The story always cuts deeper than the knife. I wince at the idea of anything entering my body. As a child, I stole quarters from my father's coat pockets. A long time ago, there was a dry beach, water frothing, impolite. I was in a cab with my sister and we were speeding down the boulevard, the ground tar-slick and gleaming, the sun so high that heat became a prayer to those below it. We rushed past this: a cluster of boys, bodies brown and long, shoulders too big for their chests. A clenched fist and two boys dropped, wrapped around each other, every part of them touching. Meryam and I are not as similar as I hoped. Do you see where this is going? I don't know why whales or elephants mourn the way they do. A new song for each death. A whole herd carrying bones for miles. Memory running deeper than it should.

OUR MOTHERS FED US WELL

After Katherine Liu

The story begins and ends here, a mouth unopen, the girl buried as she is born. The sky heaving, stars unlit. A man spills god in the humid air and they all bow their heads. Ameen. Piece by piece, the building crumbles, the stone rots. The little mosque at the end of the road, midnight, with her sister and her sister's children. Even here, she does not fit. Even here, she is a stranger. The hard cost of English, tongue betraying the skin. All the women and children clustered together like bad teeth. I don't mean to make a habit of these things, but somehow loss trails me, the people I touch turned to stone. Midnight, in the little apartment, the city and its lovers sleeping, even the stray dogs quiet, even the begging women and their empty mouths gone.

ACKNOWLEDGMENTS

Laylat Al-Qadr will appear in *SOFTBLOW's* twelfth-anniversary print edition

EVERYTHING HERE
LENA BEZAWORK GRÖNLUND

Published by Akashic Books
©2017 Lena Bezawork Grönlund

ISBN: 978-1-61775-566-8

Akashic Books
Brooklyn, New York
Twitter: @AkashicBooks
Facebook: AkashicBooks
E-mail: info@akashicbooks.com
Website: www.akashicbooks.com

African Poetry Book Fund
Prairie Schooner
University of Nebraska
110 Andrews Hall
Lincoln, Nebraska 68588

TABLE OF CONTENTS

In *Everything Here*, Lena Bezawork Grönlund renders—out of distance and color, soil and rain—a homeworld even as she writes its absence. These are poems that document transience and separation as we follow a speaker who returns, as an adult, to the place of her birth, a place someone once decided she must leave. Poem by poem, fragment by fragment, a story becomes clearer even as it remains elusive: there is a twin, a mother has died, the fright of a father's eyes, a war, 1976, the color red and the color blue, a family, Addis Ababa, wooden cars, libraries. Such a list begins to provide a historical context for the poems, though the implications and consequences of this history are always anchored by a very local, personal perspective. This said, it becomes clear that central to this work is the brutal reign of the Derg, Ethiopia's military junta in which hundreds of thousands of Ethiopian and Eritrean civilians were tortured and killed between the mid-seventies to the early nineties. And while the catalyst for the speaker's own migration is never clearly stated, the poems communicate, through silence and language, that war is at least one of the elements that has blown her and her twin into the distances from which she writes so remarkably.

In these poems personal history, silence, and the unknown are woven with nuance and honesty. Though the poems are always rendered with deep regard for their subjects, it is also true that they invite us to push against what Chimamanda Adichie calls "the single story," instead providing us with moments to suspect that "the things we know shift" ("Shift"). These shifts are enacted by the poems themselves, and by the craft decisions and routes of their maker. With effectively sparse, associative imagery, with metaphor and simile, with syntactical variation and enjambment, the poems push us out into parallel and multiple possibilities. Even a place is many places. And in Bezawork Grönlund's hands, the lyric itself becomes a place of invention and impossibility, perhaps enacting the possession and work

5

of remembering and trying to remember. In the collection's opening poem, "Come Back," she writes:

> (*We are seven years old every day*).
>   A gigantic umbrella
>   over a seven-year old hand.
>   How well it protects us.
>   How lucky we are,
>   you or me, to find it there. It is a brown
> hand holding on to the umbrella.
> I walk around on these streets where people sometimes
> shout after me.
>   I am falling now.
> (*Go back to where you were seven years ago.*) I am not
> opening my eyes.
>   Not until I am there.
> This is how it will proceed. I will keep on returning.
>   I am back here. Maybe

Gorgeously, swiftly, the poem troubles linear notions of progress and time with breathtaking intelligence and emotional sophistication. This is a poem of "I" and "we." The first-person plural describes the speaker and her twin *and* the multiple versions (through history, through memory) of those subjects. The "or" ("you or me") swiftly, subtly reminds us that while memory can possess us, memory is sometimes also the tricky terrain of "or" that offers possibilities instead of clear answers. The shouting people of this poem might be shouting shouts of recognition, or perhaps violence. The *"(Go back to where you were seven years ago.)"* might be carrying inside it the possibility of affection or taunt. In this poem, as happens so often in *Everything Here*, Bezawork Grönlund's lines are weighted with history and possibility. I read again, "I am back here. Maybe" and just as quickly as the stability of the first sentence takes hold, the "maybe" becomes sand under my feet. Even the certainty of where one stands (in place) is questioned, unraveled into simultaneity, as in, *Where else is my home? Where else might a possible self be standing? Where is my absence standing?* And so it is fitting that these poems move across the page, each one differently oriented and shaped, sometimes against the left margin or centered or against the right. Sometimes flooded with space as though with river, rain, distance, or light, sometimes dense with the black marks and implied breaths of words. In this way, Lena Bezawork Grönlund has forged a powerful and tender archive of seeking. Filled with the vulnerability of the hyphen space, or the in-between, these poems are constantly reaching *toward* understanding or the project of meaning-making. The poet is compelled to notice blue things and red things, as if creating a lineage of color. Red: thread, machines, neon lights, red terror. Blue: sky, the ink of letters sent by the speaker's mother and father, branches, marches, machines. She does not make meaning (for us) out of this collection of color, but instead reveals something far more interesting: the tendencies of this specific mind at work noticing, collecting, and arranging what has been found, what has been left. Other times language is silence. And sometimes it is a portal, as in this moment in "Song" when the speaker is looking at the blue writing of her mother and father:

> These words
> should speak to me,
> but there is only silence
> here. I never learned
> my native alphabet.
> These Amharic letters
> may as well be blots
> of ink to me,
> and suddenly
> a forceful fluid form

rushes, like magma,
to battle those solid
words. —*All my life*
I haven't been back.
As if someone poured
coffee over them, they are
loose now in shape,
dissolving into oceanic ink,
pooling on my floor.
Up from there the words rise
in petite tin forms, smiling
and pointing at me.
—*That's a long time.*
With my mouth first I fall
gently toward a dark surface,
tasting warm fluids.
The rest of me rushing
into a fluid form
out of which I step out clean

It is important to me that the sudden transformation of these letters into fluid is likened to someone pouring coffee over the marks. It is important to me that coffee is wed with transformation here, as coffee is what our people gather around in the ritual of sharing, talk, and closeness at homecomings and social visits. It is also important to me that this speaker falls toward the letters with her mouth, "With my mouth first I fall / gently toward a dark surface," and that the falling happens differently than most falling. It is a falling toward a surface, toward an air. Suddenly it is a birth I am witnessing. A birth, I am sure.

In *Everything Here* we have the chance to read a poet well acquainted with the effortful work of trying to see, across space and time, some trace of home, however fragmented and shifting. The speaker of the poems searches for traces of herself through the implied distance of photographs and letters, poring over faces, postures, books. Bezawork Grönlund's poems are not poems of resolution or arrival. These poems reveal a project utterly profound and rare: the cultivation of a critical imaginative strategy in the face of distance and loss. These are gleaming poems of effort and possibility.

COME BACK

As I remember it every thread is in red.

       As I remember it is not how it was.

       Sometimes words can go through the body

       just to come back,

       maybe a few hours later,

       sometimes years, sometimes seconds.

                 When you are a child.

(*I am a brown child with a big umbrella.*) An old umbrella,

an umbrella that always stands upside down

in the umbrella stand in the corner of the hall until you or I find it.

(*We are seven years old every day.*)

       A gigantic umbrella

       over a seven-year-old hand.

       How well it protects us.

       How lucky we are,

       you or me, to find it there. It is a brown hand holding on

to the umbrella.

I walk around on these streets where people sometimes shout after me.

       I am falling now.

(*Go back to where you were seven years ago.*) I am not opening my eyes.

       Not until I am there.

This is how it will proceed. I will keep on returning.

       I am back here. Maybe

if I stand still

on this spot

long enough

these threads in me will find their way down and stay there,

again

more of me,

again

here. I am standing completely still on the street.
I close my eyes. The air does not move. I wrap my shawl
over my face,
threads pull downward, remain here. (*It has been decided.*)
This is where I came from.
This is where I stay.

RIVERS

I can smell the dust here.
Maybe that is why
I keep coming back.
Libraries are the same
everywhere. Today the sun
is close to the window.
I push my hand against
the glass. Cold. Outside
blue sky, clouds move softly.
Leaves in masses whirl
like crowds of refugees
driven away by war. Inside
I turn pages following
photographs of the New Flower[1],
watching out for someone
who looks like me
more than once.
I am there, a girl looking out
from behind the corner
of a fading house.
Then there is nothing
but this building,
the blue sky,
wings flapping in my mind.
Eshu, introducer
of chance and accident,
I imagine him
standing still, lurking

---

1 Addis Ababa, the capital of Ethiopia, means "new flower" in Ethiopia's national language Amharic.

13

inside the warm air of Ethiopia,
hovering over that house
in which my mother,
never having gone to school,
swept floors,
seeing to it that my father,
the student,
started repairing the walls.
Eshu brought them together.
That is how they met.
How they came to part,
my father has never said.
"—Eshu, the wind blows stronger outside.
Will she be able to stand?"
Raindrops fall.
These pages are dry.
She is there again.
The same face more than once.
Eshu is watching her.

SONG

Spread and illuminated
under my desk lamp,
pages of old and new
letters, blue longhand
staring fiercely at me
where I sit in my gray
swingable chair into late-
night hours. —*How long
has it been since
you've been back home?*
The hands who wrote
these lines are my mother's
and father's. These words
should speak to me,
but there is only silence
here. I never learned
my native alphabet.
These Amharic letters
may as well be blots
of ink to me,
and suddenly
a forceful fluid form
rushes, like magma,
to battle those solid
words. —*All my life
I haven't been back.*
As if someone poured
coffee over them, they are
loose now in shape,

dissolving into oceanic ink,
pooling on my floor.
Up from there the words rise
in petite tin forms, smiling
and pointing at me.
—*That's a long time.*
With my mouth first I fall
gently toward a dark surface,
tasting warm fluids.
The rest of me rushing
into a fluid form
out of which I step out clean
as from a shower
for the first time as an Ethiopian,
—*Too long*
playing marbles in alleys
of city streets
in Addis Ababa,
running with my siblings
in between metal shacks
and big hotels.
Chasing cool shadow,
sand clouds rise
in between and after us.
I stop to see dust
falling down like a curtain,
catching breath
and perceiving among people
a mother and a father
walking closer.

MERCATO, ADDIS

                red bicycles

                blue houses
                red bicycles

I dream
of blue houses

            red bicycles

WE HAD TO BE SOLDIERS BACK THEN

Ka hullum belay, Abiotu

Your father saved my life,

his friend begins.
We all had to be soldiers

back then. We weren't
good soldiers,

but we were soldiers.
My family

on my father's side
is circled

around a table
close to Lake Ziwai;

a lake
that has no end,

no space
between the sky

and the lake,
between a name

and a thing.

We'd wish

we could keep
the peace in that;

just the sight
and the peace in that.

They talk of the spirits,
after and during

Qey Shibir,
how they saw them

disappear
in large flocks

like crowds
of birds.

One of us
is missing—

Anteneh,
stationed

forever
by the border.

I'm lucky,

I don't know war.

We had
wooden soldiers.

We had
a wooden land.

This whole
country was

a battlefield,
a battlefield,

my father says,
leaning forward,

whispering,
I let the prisoners

that I could, go.

THE TRACK

He is just a young man.
He is just a young man
by a steel track.
He wants the streets
to be more than streets.
The Italian boulevard
the Italians quickly built
to be more than a boulevard.
He wants his dreams to be more than just dreams.
The city more than a city.

He has such high,
admirable ideals.
It is an unjust time.
The emperor
is such a powerful
man. The Derg
and the military
the most violent
letdown.

My father's voice
is clear, tender.
He wants to tell this story quickly, it's still a dangerous
thing to do, he points to the window, says—*The way
the rain falls this time of year it reminds me of the first
year before we lost hope.*
He looks to the side,
he looks back, says everything became an illusion like

the red
in the neon light,
like the red terror.

NEW-GENERATION AFRICAN POETS

A CHAPBOOK BOX SET

NNE

AN INTRODUCTION IN TWO MOVEMENTS BY
KWAME DAWES & CHRIS ABANI

Published by Akashic Books
©2017 Kwame Dawes and Chris Abani

ISBN for full box set: 978-1-61775-540-8
Library of Congress Control Number for full box set: 2016953895

Akashic Books
Brooklyn, New York
Twitter: @AkashicBooks
Facebook: AkashicBooks
E-mail: info@akashicbooks.com
Website: www.akashicbooks.com

African Poetry Book Fund
Prairie Schooner
University of Nebraska
110 Andrews Hall
Lincoln, Nebraska 68588

For Lorna,
Sena, Kekeli, and Akua,
Mama the Great,
and the tribe: Gwyneth, Kojo, Aba, Adjoa, Kojovi.
K.D.

*

For Daphne, Michael, Mark, Charles, Greg, Stella—my family.
I love you.
C.A.

NEW-GENERATION AFRICAN POETS (NNE)

Introduction by Kwame Dawes and Chris Abani

CONTENTS OF BOX SET

NEW-GENERATION AFRICAN POETS (NNE)

Introduction in Two Movements
by Kwame Dawes and Chris Abani

PART ONE

The Body As an Alien and Dangerous Entity

Perhaps the first thing that anyone will see when considering
this box set will be the artwork that graces all the covers of these
chapbooks and the box itself. The work is that of a remarkable
Eritrean artist, the late Ficre Ghebreyesus, whose art we have
been able to secure through the generosity and solidarity of his
wife Elizabeth Alexander and his family. The compelling fasci-
nation with the body, the African body, that marks his art, seems
to rhyme perfectly with the poetry that is collected here. Our
project is enhanced tremendously by having the work of such an
important and accomplished artist. In the end, the art lives on in
beautiful and meaningful ways, through the conversations that it
has with the work of other artists.

We invited about thirty-five poets to submit manuscripts
for this year's chapbook box set. This is an annual ritual that we
are committed to carrying until we arrive at the tenth year of
publishing the chapbooks of a new generation of African poets.
Each year, the task gets more and more difficult. The quality of
the manuscripts is extremely impressive. The range of the work

we are getting is equally striking, representing poets living in Africa and those of African heritage living in the recent African diaspora. More and more people are sending us the names of poets who they believe would do well to be considered for the series, and so making the selection has become a greater and greater challenge for Chris Abani and myself—but it is a challenge that we welcome. It confirms a hunch we have had for a while that given the possibility of a thoughtful, well-edited publishing entity for their work, the African poets will emerge. We are not *discovering* poets. This should be clear from any brief look at the poets we are publishing here. All of them are serious writers who have been engaged with the world of publishing, having had individual poems published in literary journals and anthologies around the world, and having won fellowships, awards, and prizes for their writing. For many who follow the writing of poets of color or who pay attention to the spoken word scene, some of the names listed here will not be strange at all. A few are at the final stages of putting together their debut collection of poems, and others can be read online. Yet, for many of them, their presence in this singular gathering of African poets is an important step, and there is something extremely exciting about seeing the ways in which they have engaged this complex idea of Africanness with their work.

There are some striking features of this year's box set. Firstly, despite our efforts to keep the number of chapbooks collected here to seven or eight, we were unable to reduce the number to less than ten. Indeed, a few of the collections that are not included may well have been included had we the resources to do so. Secondly, it will be clear that of the ten poets collected here, nine of them are women. On the surface this seems remarkable, but while we have not tried to understand why this is the case, we welcome it as an exciting development in African poetry, which has, for many decades, been wholly dominated by male voices. Finally, a significant proportion of the selections here represent poets who either currently live outside of Africa or spend their time moving back and forth between Africa and the rest of the world. The African Poetry Book Fund has been working hard to maintain a pair of core principles in the work that we do that may seem contradictory, but in practice prove to be necessary ways of approaching the work that we do. On one hand, we have sought to give as much attention to finding and supporting the work of poets who are living and working in African countries where many of the opportunities for publication and formal mentorship are limited. To this end, we have developed a fairly exciting network of partners all across the continent and this has proven to be an exciting development for us. At the same time, we have sought to recognize that so many of the poets from Africa have found homes outside of the continent for reasons that may have little to do with their poetry careers, but have more to do with the complex circumstances of life that have led to our people being a people of migration and transcultural movement. And we have held to the view that many of these poets living outside of Africa have had an equally difficult time finding communities that share their own experience and may even understand their distinctive aesthetics and concerns as poets. By tackling these two goals at the same time, we have been enacting the larger principles of Pan-Africanism with the caution of not attempting to totalize the experience of African people.

But here is the truth: notwithstanding these necessary considerations of geography, culture, and gender, what we have been thrilled by is the quality of the poetry that is collected here.

There is a startling intelligence running through each of these collections, but beyond it all, I have left this process of working closely with manuscript after manuscript with a sense that the singular thing that connects these books is the way in which these poets root the emotional and intellectual explorations in the body—the body as an alien and dangerous entity that is negotiating its presence in a world that is sometimes hostile, sometimes welcoming, but always forcing the poet to resist erasure and invisibility.

I decided to create a collage of these instances in the collection that continue to remind me of the varied concerns of these poets and, at the same time, the collective.

In Lena Bezawork Grönlund's *Everything Here*, she describes the legacy of the bodies of her parents on her body in an alien Swedish landscape: "I look at him / with her thin shoulders / against the wall, his thin face, / his startled look, and her deep lines / under my eyes." ("Still Life")

In Famia Nkansa's collection *Sabbatical*, she explores the theme of visibility and invisibility: "do you see this me, more than I could even be, or the me that me and everyone else would see if we only took the energy to look hard enough?" ("it is from my need to matter than I ask you this")

In her poem "mom's on fire," in her collection *i know how to fix myself*, Ashley Makue observes, "my mother is a war zone / they don't tell her that / these men that pee in her / and leave with gunpowder in their chests."

Victoria Adukwei Bulley's collection, *Girl B*, is filled with exquisite transgressions of the body like this: "Hair coming down past your breasts like confetti. Your straighter teeth, your stripped upper lip (recoiling still), your clean, dark complexion. Lean thighs, or the gap between them. The grasp of your jeans at you like a lover that you'd like to leave, exposing the gap." ("Girl")

And here, in Chimwemwe Undi's poem "On Sickness" (*The Habitual Be*), she invokes Lucille Clifton's defiance of various enemies of the black woman's body: "The dark perfection of this body / is disallowed from cracking. / Won't you celebrate with me, / nonwhite & woman, how / I can but may not name / the thing I know is / trying to kill me."

In Yasmin Belkhyr's provocative exploration of religion and piety in her poem "Eid Al-Adha," she engages notions of the body and the violence it is capable of. She writes: "There are so many bodies of mine that I haven't claimed yet. So many versions, so many lives. Fat purple figs and all that. When I speak of bodies, I mean: I'm afraid of mine. When I speak of bodies, I mean: I wonder what yours is capable of. When I speak of bodies, I mean: there is too much inside of me . . ." (*Bone Light*)

Mary-Alice Daniel contemplates what we end up doing with the body in science and in the world of exhibitions, which calls to mind what was done to Ota Benga at the turn of the last century: "You can do to a body a lot of things. / A feature in *Smithsonian* on cannibals makes me hungry. // I'm learning so much—they use bodies as ritual snacks, / eating everything but teeth, hair, and penis." ("Blood for the Blood God")

For Chekwube O. Danladi, the body's capacity for pleasure and the exploration of profound sensuality is directly connected to its capacity to be broken, its unsettling vulnerability. In "Communion" she writes: "No one has a body that cannot be broken. / I shatter beneath a windowsill, separate as fruit / for provender: pomelo breasts, / lemondrop melon ass, a head / of ripened cantaloupe." (*Take Me Back*)

In the elusively elliptical prose poems in her chapbook *sugah. lump. prayer*, Momtaza Mehri occasionally anchors the reader in a meditation on a subject that is full of sensual and psychic complexity, as in her poem about the body, "In that order." Again, vulnerability is tempered by agency and desire: "my body gives way to salt gives way to a bruised telephone line gives way to honeyed mahalibya tones gives way to the corner of your mouth gives way to I can smell it on you gives way to that russet-mustached soldier on the cheapest stamp gives way to the letters gives way to burnt sukkar gives way to caramel ripple gives way to slipping on cotton socks gives way to slippery men gives way to // dissolve."

Finally, in Ejiọfọr Ugwu's *The Book of God*, we find the poem "Magun," which beautifully renders mutation of the man's body into a vessel—a boat that must traverse various waterways. "I am a sea child. / I armpitted my paddle, / my boat on my head, / and set out for the sea under. / What is it with me and / the life of swamps?"

Each of these chapbooks has been introduced by poets of great accomplishment and insight in their own right. It is a sign of the generosity of the community that is taking shape around the African Poetry Book Fund that we have little trouble finding poets of significant standing willing to write insightful and generous introductions to each of these chapbooks. Thus it is important to thank Karen McCarthy Woolf, Ladan Osman, Honorée Fannone Jeffers, Patricia Jabbeh Wesley, Tsisi Jaji, Matthew Shenoda, Aracelis Girmay, and Tijan M. Sallah for their work in support of these poets.

Finally, managing this complex project has been the inimitable Ashley Strosnider, whose editorial eye and brilliant administrative skill and insight have been essential to the success of this project.

—*Kwame Dawes*

PART TWO
The Poem is a Body and the Body a Poem

"Every story I create, creates me. I write to create myself."
—Octavia E. Butler

The poem is a body and the body a poem. This is not something I can prove, nor even something that is necessarily true, but it does have the ring of truth about it. This is a more intuitive relationship but one I think we are all fairly conversant with and one with which most poetry lovers will agree. The one true topography of self we can chart, navigate, and map is the body. The visible self leads to the more ethereal and ineffable parts of self, the parts that poetry tries to give symbolic meaning to, to invoke that presence. And if we look closer, we see that it's not just that language gives the body presence, shape, resistance, love, affirmation, and intervention. And it is not just that the bodies of particular poets give their language a certain shape and definition, but rather that in the end, our particular idiosyncratic languages are our bodies. We exist only in the space of that language, and we use it to move a craft forward, to draw and redraw the limits of the self, both internal and external. We can argue that this is poetry's true power, to shape reality—and that is truly what power is: the choice and ability to redraw and recast our personal narratives.

No body has been more colonized, commoditized, traumatized, and dehumanized than the black body, and by definition, the African body. From the earliest ways that Europe plundered our cultures, histories, sciences, discoveries, and resources to the most recent holocaust of slavery, the legacy of these violences is still being fought the world over. So it has been particularly important to offer space and staging ground for these reclamations of the body.

From the ways that global capitalism and racism, patriarchy, and the other forms of repression have restricted and attempted to own and commodify the black body, the poems and poets represented here (and in our previous box sets) are a vanguard and growing archive of resistance and rearticulation of self. So geography, culture, and gender have become the hallmarks of these poems.

One of the things Kwame Dawes and I have struggled to maintain is the ratio of diaspora to continental poets. This is a struggle because diaspora poets do have better access to workshops and other spaces of craft education and are often better poised at the submission stage to be better poets.

As Kwame has pointed out, it is a difficult call to make because while we recognize the need for the curating we have undertaken, we are mindful of its dangers. We are mindful not to try to referee who is an African, or what constitutes or doesn't constitute Africanness. We worry that our curating will leave out voices that are vital to a more rounded African poetry archive either stylistically, aesthetically, linguistically, geographically, or in terms of gender. This is always a worry for the curator/editor; we know on the one hand that we are, intentionally or not, creating a representational archive while desperately seeking to create an all-inclusive and encompassing one. We don't want to be seen as saying *this* is African poetry, but rather, here are some of the new conversations happening in this art form, within this particular cultural moment, by these poets of African descent living on or off the continent.

You see, not only is the poem the body, or at least the simulacrum of the body, the book (or the poetry collection, which is not always a book anymore) is itself the body, maybe of the poet, but definitely of the poet's imagination. What we are beginning to see emerge, with this archive, is definitely a body. It is a body of work that is attempting to define something already and always in flux: a growing culture, a changing culture, an expanding zeitgeist, and an ever-evolving moment. This body of African poetry is exciting, and like all true simulacra, it has outgrown its original code, it has become its own consciousness. We see this body, this ineffable self in dialogue with itself—through time, with all the poets that have come before, many of whom are still being shaken off for the poet to find an original voice; but also, this new generation of poets is in dialogue with itself, the poems speaking to each other, thus these poets are reforming and repositioning the archive from within, causing it to grow and expand in interesting ways.

The process itself, of selecting these poets, can be equally frustrating and humbling. Frustrating on many levels, because we have to turn down so many with so much potential, partly because the editing we have to do to make them publication-ready is beyond our current scope (and we are trying to remedy that by developing workshops to be taken to different countries on the continent). And we have to turn down so many good poets because we can only choose ten. It is humbling because of the sheer array of talent on display by poets who are so early in their careers.

And so we are back once more to the idea of the body—the alien body of blackness at risk in the West where it sometimes settles, the familiar body of blackness at home that is also at risk from internal and external forces of homogenization. But the most important thing that we see developing is that whatever these forces are that are being brought to bear on these bodies, the poetic instinct, aesthetic, and political enactments here are working against forgetting, erasure, sentimentality, nostalgia, and anomie; instead, they are leaning into reinscription, reenactments of prosody and language, and a redrawing of the body both at stasis and in flux, an idea Homi Bhabha would certainly love.

Kwame has already sampled the poems to show the spaces of resistance, slippage, and redefinition, allowing for the individuality of concerns and yet pointing assuredly to a growing archive, a body, in dialogue. If this is where we find ourselves at this time, nearly fifty chapbooks in, then we are in a good place.

—*Chris Abani*

KWAME DAWES is the author of eighteen collections of poetry, most recently *Duppy Conqueror,* as well as two novels and numerous anthologies and plays. He has won Pushcart Prizes, a Guggenheim Fellowship, an Emmy, and was the 2013 awardee of the Paul Engel Prize. At the University of Nebraska–Lincoln, he is a Chancellor's Professor of English and Glenna Luschei Editor of *Prairie Schooner.* Dawes is the associate poetry editor at Peepal Tree Press, the series editor of the University of South Carolina Poetry Series, and the founding director of the African Poetry Book Fund. He teaches in the Pacific MFA Program and is director of the biennial Calabash International Literary Festival.

CHRIS ABANI's prose includes *The Secret History of Las Vegas*, *Song for Night*, *The Virgin of Flames*, *Becoming Abigail*, *GraceLand*, and *Masters of the Board*. His poetry collections are *Sanctificum*, *There Are No Names for Red*, *Feed Me the Sun*, *Hands Washing Water*, *Dog Woman*, *Daphne's Lot*, and *Kalakuta Republic*. He holds a BA in English, an MA in gender and culture, an MA in English, and a PhD in literature and creative writing. Abani is the recipient of a PEN USA Freedom to Write Award, a Prince Claus Award, a Lannan Literary Fellowship, a California Book Award, a Hurston/Wright Legacy Award, a PEN Beyond Margins Award, a PEN/Hemingway Award, and a Guggenheim Award. Born in Nigeria, he is currently Board of Trustees Professor of English at Northwestern University in Chicago.

FICRE GHEBREYESUS (cover artist) was born in Asmara, Eritrea. He left the country as a political refugee and lived in Sudan, Italy, and Germany before coming to the United States, where he earned his undergraduate degree and worked as a humanitarian activist on behalf of Eritrean independence and ongoing relief issues. He studied painting at the Art Students' League and printmaking at the Bob Blackburn Printmaking Workshop, both in New York City. He later studied at Yale University, where he earned his MFA and was awarded the Carol Schlossberg Prize for Excellence in Painting at graduation.

Ghebreyesus lived in New Haven for almost thirty years with his wife Elizabeth Alexander and their sons Solomon and Simon. From 1992–2008, he was executive chef and coowner with his brothers of the immensely popular Caffe Adulis that brought creative Eritrean cuisine to New Haven and New York City. In the last years of his life he dedicated his work time solely to his art. He died unexpectedly in April 2012.

*Also available in the New-Generation African Poets Chapbook Box Set Series
from Akashic Books and the African Poetry Book Fund*

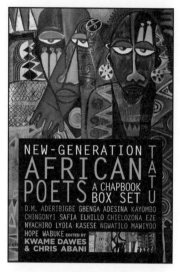

NEW-GENERATION AFRICAN POETS: A CHAPBOOK BOX SET (TATU)

edited by Kwame Dawes and Chris Abani
9-piece chapbook box set, slip-cased, shrinkwrapped, $29.95

FEATURING CHAPBOOKS BY: D.M. Aderibigbe, Gbenga Adesina, Kayombo Chingonyi, Safia Elhillo, Chielozona Eze, Nyachiro Lydia Kasese, Ngwatilo Mawiyoo, and Hope Wabuke, and an introduction chapbook by Kwame Dawes and Chris Abani.

"*New-Generation African Poets* is an ambitious, vital project that delivers exactly what it promises . . . As a group, the chapbooks dispel stereotypes about African writing. They also illustrate what editors Dawes and Abani note about the many ways poets can understand or redefine their ties to Africa. These insights are poignant and valuable, especially at a time when millions around the globe find themselves somewhere between new countries and ancestral lands they've left behind." —*Washington Post*

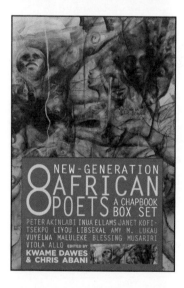

EIGHT NEW-GENERATION AFRICAN POETS: A CHAPBOOK BOX SET

edited by Kwame Dawes and Chris Abani
9-piece chapbook box set, slip-cased, shrinkwrapped, $29.95

FEATURING CHAPBOOKS BY: Peter Akinlabi, Viola Allo, Inua Ellams, Janet Kofi-Tsekpo, Liyou Mesfin Libsekal, Amy Lukau, Vuyelwa Maluleke, and Blessing Musariri, and an introduction chapbook by Kwame Dawes and Chris Abani.

"Each of these chapbooks is so worthy of praise and attention that it is not possible to do them justice in the space afforded this review. They deserve, and hopefully will receive, the specific and individual attention of critics and readers, and their authors deserve to enjoy long and noted careers." —*Untucked Magazine*

"The beauty of this collection is not just in the interplay of cover art and text, of preface and poem, but especially in its overall optimistic effect." —*Africa in Words*

The New-Generation African Poets Chapbook Box Set series is an annual project of the African Poetry Book Fund—established through the generosity of Laura and Robert F.X. Sillerman and published in collaboration with Akashic Books—which seeks to identify the best poetry written by African authors working today, with a special focus on those who have not yet published their first full-length book of poetry.

Available from our website and at online and brick & mortar bookstores everywhere.
www.akashicbooks.com | info@akashicbooks.com
For more information about the African Poetry Book Fund, please visit africanpoetrybf.unl.edu.

Seven New Generation African Poets
edited by Kwame Dawes and Chris Abani
8-piece chapbook box set, slip-cased, shrinkwrapped, $29.95
The inaugural box set in the New-Generation African Poets Chapbook
Box Set series. Slapering Hol Press (2014)

Madman at Kilifi
by Clifton Gachagua, 78 pages, paperback, $14.95
Winner of the Sillerman First Book Prize for African Poets.
University of Nebraska Press (2014)

The Promise of Hope: New and Selected Poems
by Kofi Awoonor, 336 pages, paperback, $19.95
A beautifully edited collection of some of Awoonor's most arresting
work spanning almost fifty years.
University of Nebraska Press (2014)

The Kitchen-Dweller's Testimony
by Ladan Osman, 108 pages, paperback, $15.95
Winner of the Sillerman First Book Prize for African Poets.
University of Nebraska Press (2015)

Fuchsia
by Mahtem Shiferraw, 108 pages, paperback, $15.95
Winner of the Sillerman First Book Prize for African Poets.
University of Nebraska Press (2016)

Gabriel Okara: Collected Poems
by Gabriel Okara, 168 pages, paperback, $19.95
Gabriel Okara, a prize-winning author whose literary career spans six
decades, is rightly hailed as the elder statesman of Nigerian literature.
University of Nebraska Press (2016)

Also available in the African Poetry Book Fund Series

Logotherapy
by Mukoma Wa Ngugi, 96 pages, paperback, $15.95
Written as a tribute to family, place, and bodily awareness, Mukoma Wa Ngugi's poems speak of love, war, violence, language, immigration, and exile.
University of Nebraska Press (2016)

When the Wanderers Come Home
by Patricia Jabbeh Wesley, 126 pages, paperback, $15.95
A woman's story about being an exile, a survivor, an outsider in her own country—a cry for the Africa that is being lost in wars across the continent, creating more wanderers and world citizens.
University of Nebraska Press (2016)

Forthcoming from the African Poetry Book Fund Series

The January Children by Safia Elhillo (2017)

Beating the Graves by Tsitsi Ella Jaji (2017)

After the Ceremonies: New and Selected Poems
by Ama Ata Aidoo (2017)

In a Language That You Know by Len Verway (2017)

Think of Lampedusa by Josué Guébo, translated by Todd Fredson (2017)

Under the helm of series editor Kwame Dawes, the African Poetry Book Series seeks to discover and highlight works of African poetry with a wide-ranging scope—from classic works to modern and contemporary voices. The greatest challenge facing African poetry in English is a lack of access to both classic works and the stream of works from new African writers. Currently there is no press in the United States, or elsewhere, that devotes itself entirely to the publication of African poetry written in English. This series looks to rectify this gap and also collect works of classic African poetry that have otherwise been forgotten.

With the help of an Editorial Board made up of gifted and internationally regarded poets, Kwame Dawes looks to publish two to three new titles per year.

Available from the Universtiy of Nebraska Press website
and at online and brick & mortar bookstores everywhere.
University of Nebraska Press | 1111 Lincoln Mall | Lincoln, NE 68588-0630
U.S. Orders and Customer Service: 1-800-848-6224
U.S. Fax Orders and Customer Service: 1-800-272-6817
Foreign Orders and Customer Service: 1-919-966-7449
Customer Service E-mail: customerservice@longleafservices.org
Journals Customer Service E-mail: journals@unl.edu

For more information about the African Poetry Book Fund, please visit africanpoetrybf.unl.edu.